THE
DIVORCING
CHRISTIAN

THE DIVORCING CHRISTIAN

LEWIS R. RAMBO

ABINGDON PRESS • NASHVILLE

THE DIVORCING CHRISTIAN

Copyright © 1983 by Abingdon Press

Library of Congress Cataloging in Publication Data

RAMBO, LEWIS R. (Lewis Ray), 1943-
  The divorcing Christian.
  Includes bibliographical references.
  1. Divorce—Religious aspects—Christianity.
I. Title.
BT707.R35   1983   284.8'4   83-6361

ISBN 0-687-10994-9

Manufactured by the Parthenon Press at
Nashville, Tennessee, United States of America

To
Harold and Gwen Rambo
my parents, who gave me life and loving support

Anna Catherine Rambo
my daughter, who gives me joy and hope

Contents

PREFACE

Ecclesiastes 3:1-8 serves as a biblical framework for the chapters of this book. The range of human experience, the rhythm of brokenness and deliverance, sorrow and joy, serve to remind us that the structure and dynamics of our lives are rooted in God's creation and design.

The Divorcing Christian emerged, as you will see, from my own personal experience. The first draft of the book was written in twelve days. In August of 1982 I gave three presentations to a group of divorced members of the Church of Christ in Texas. Their response so inspired me that I returned to California and produced this book. Before those presentations and before writing this book, I had read only three books on divorce. That may sound irresponsible to some people, but for someone who had always read books to solve his problems, it was a major breakthrough. For the first time in my life I gave my own personal experience priority.

In March of 1981 I began reading *Creative Divorce* (New York: Signet, 1973) by Mel Krantzler. The first two chapters proved to be so accurate in their descriptions of my condition that I could not tolerate the book. In May of 1981 I read Richard Schickel's *Singled Out* (New York: Viking Press, 1981). If you are wondering how it is possible for me to remember the dates of reading particular books, I should inform you that one of the benefits of being compulsive is that I write the date at the end of every chapter or article I read.

Even though I had agreed to make three presentations on divorce to a group of divorced Christians in Texas long before August, it was really only the week before that I began preparations in earnest. The catalyst for my thinking was a splendid book by William Bridges entitled *Transitions: Making Sense of Life's Changes* (Reading, Mass.: Addison-Wesley, 1980). That marvelous book seemed to remove the barriers to my thoughts and feelings on divorce. I completed that book on August 21, 1982, and then returned to Krantzler's *Creative Divorce*. My pain was not as raw as the year before, and I found myself affirming most of Krantzler's insights. After the conference in Texas (August 27-29, 1982), I completed Robert A. Raines' *Going Home* (San Francisco: Harper and Row, 1979). The intensity of Raines' theological reflections liberated me to think theologically on the various dimensions of divorce for the Christian. In a remarkable burst of energy I wrote the first 91 pages of the first draft of this book between September 9 and September 17. While waiting at the airport for a friend delayed for eight hours, I read Jim Smoke's *Growing Through Divorce* (Irvine, Cal.: Harvest House, 1976). That book confirmed many of my own thoughts that I had written in the manuscript. A position of the radical forgiveness of God for the divorced person was confirmed by my reading of Larry Richards' *Remarriage: A Healing Gift from God* (Waco, Texas, 1981).

During the process of revising the book and planning a course on divorce counseling, I have begun to read the literature on the subject. Even though my book is not meant to be a handbook on divorce, at appropriate points in the book I will make suggestions for further reading.

Many friends deserve a special word of gratitude for their empathy, compassion, humor, faith, and support. The list, if I included everyone, would fill several pages. The following people have given me love and kindness to an extraordinary degree: David

Glick, Jill Martinez, Evelyn Brouwer, Ted Stein, Warren Lee, Roy Fairchild, Marsue Harris, Barbara Pruitt, Carol Chesnin, Linda Peterson, and Julie and Lloyd Patterson.

My colleagues at the San Francisco Theological Seminary and the Graduate Theological Union were gracious to me during the divorce. Time off for writing was provided by President Arnold Come and Dean Browne Barr. Splendid secretarial services were provided by Loel Millar, Kathy Taylor, and Sandy Mihal.

The people at the Church of Christ in San Rafael, California, were constant in their support of me. I thank them for allowing me to express myself candidly in my teaching and preaching. I also thank them for sponsoring workshops for divorced Christians. Within the Churches of Christ, no one has done more for divorced Christians than Anthony L. Ash. It was his invitation to give three presentations that were the original inspiration for this book.

Many people read the manuscript of this book. Ruth A. Fox helped me transform the first draft into the second draft. Her skill and vitality helped me persevere. James Dittes, Martin Marty, Robert Lee, James McClendon, Carroll Saussy, and many others offered encouragement. Of course, I alone am responsible for any remaining faults.

CHAPTER I

FACING THE CRISIS

For everything there is a season, and a time for every matter under heaven:
a time to be born, and a time to die;
a time to plant, and a time to pluck up what is planted;
a time to kill, and a time to heal;
a time to break down, and a time to build up;
a time to weep, and a time to laugh;
a time to mourn, and a time to dance;
a time to cast away stones, and a time to gather stones together;
a time to embrace, and a time to refrain from embracing;
a time to seek, and a time to lose;
a time to keep, and a time to cast away;
a time to rend, and a time to sew;
a time to keep silence, and a time to speak;
a time to love, and a time to hate;
a time for war, and a time for peace.

Ecclesiastes 3:1-8   RSV

For the Christian, divorce is an excruciating, complicated problem. The traditions of the church and the sometimes ruthless conscience of the individual join forces to wreak havoc on and in us. Divorce is a form of psychological amputation and mutilation—some would say death—which is painful for everyone, but the Christian carries the added burden and balm of the faith, which both condemns and consoles. In this book, I will explore the traumatic experience of divorce from the inside out, to give you who are divorced and are trying to deal with the fact some ideas about the internal processes, the patterns of thoughts and feelings you are experiencing. And for those who seek to minister to divorced Christians, the book will suggest some principles and guidelines to help you understand the needs of those you are counseling and to facilitate your work together, so that they and you may find deeper faith in the process.

This is not a Pollyanna book. Some unpleasant things will be discussed, and those who have not been through the experience may not believe how thoroughly divorce can distort life. Some will say that Christians should not feel or say or do these things, but I would contend that the Christian—even one from a rigid or legalistic form of the faith—does feel and say and do them, and has to acknowledge and deal with them. The book is not directed to Christians only, but since I am from that tradition, my struggles will reflect that point of view.

The book is written almost exclusively from personal experience, and much of it is autobiographical. I am given courage to write this way because, from deep friendships with other divorced people, I have found that what Carl Rogers says is true: "That which is most personal is most universal." The viewpoint of a divorced Christian may seem narrow, but there are millions of people in the United States who claim to be devoted Christians. This is not such a small group. My experience may not parallel yours exactly, but I have tried to be candid and speak as a Christian who has struggled with divorce himself, and whose struggles will be similar, at least, to yours. When I say "we" in this book, I'm not speaking to you from some objective editorial height: I mean "we." I think there is something universal in what to me is most personal; I hope you will read the book picturing us sitting together talking over our common problems, as I have sat and talked with many other divorced Christians. And I hope in doing so you may find some empathy, comfort, challenge, and healing.

I am writing for you who have already gone through a divorce. The book does not advocate divorce for Christians, but seeks to deal with the problems of Christians once divorce has happened to them. Other books need to be written to help prevent divorce and to explore the theology of divorce and remarriage. This one is a survival manual for someone from a Christian background, whether Protestant, Roman Catholic, or nondenominational. Details of teaching may vary from one group to another, but the styles of dealing with the problems related to divorce and the resulting guilt, shame, and possibility for healing are similar. Divorce is rampant in our entire society, and churches can no longer claim that "good" Christians are exempt.

Finally, I want the book to deal with divorce in a biblical and realistic manner. It grew out of not only my personal experience, but also numerous conversations with divorced Christians from diverse backgrounds, as well as people with no religious affiliation or theological commitments. The sharing and the writing have been therapeutic for me. The divorce has been the occasion for conversion. I wouldn't recommend divorce on that basis, but I am glad that spiritual renewal is possible in the midst of perplexity, guilt, shame, failure, and brokenness.

It's "Normal" to be "Crazy"

You should understand at the outset—if you haven't yet discovered or admitted it—that it is "normal" to be "crazy" during a divorce. After completion of the manuscript I found a marvelous book which describes the typical reaction to divorce: *Crazy Time: Surviving Divorce* by Abigail Trafford (New York: Harper & Row, 1982). Anyone who is "normal" in such a time of crisis is the really "crazy" person. Degrees of stress and the severity of one's sense of crisis may vary with the people and the situation. Divorce comes for some after years of struggle and discussion and a final mutual decision to terminate the marriage. In other cases, one of the partners suddenly departs quite unexpectedly. In others, a husband or wife discovers the spouse's unfaithfulness, triggering a major upheaval of home and family. But, however slowly or suddenly the crisis develops, people tend to regress to lower levels of functioning during a divorce.

We are overwhelmed with many problems at the same time. After all, there is more to divorce than "simply" the rejection of another person. There are money problems, legal problems, child-care problems, disdain of friends, strained relationships with our own parents, and on and on. During divorce, we question the fundamental bases of our very life, and we have no solid ground on which to stand. Or so we feel at the time. Our normal modes of coping no longer operate because we've already deployed all those strategies in trying to keep the marriage together—only to find, in the end, that "there's nothing I can do." The devastation is more than some people can bear.

Christians have some added problems. We may find ourselves labeled with the stigma of "sin." Some churches tend to be very harsh both on the issue of divorce and on church members who resort to it. Sometimes we have nowhere to turn because most of our friends are Christians who reject our action, so our sense of isolation grows. In addition, some of our churches and friends tell us, "good Christians" do not have emotional problems (remember, you're "crazy"!) and "good Christians" certainly never get a divorce. Feeling rejected by the spouse and perhaps by other family members, we bear the additional burden of the church's disapproval: if our faith were deep enough, we wouldn't have emotional disturbances like this; we ought to have "the peace that passes understanding" and face the pain of divorce more stoically.

Isolation, disapproval, and—most deeply and intensely—guilt haunt us. Every Christian, especially one from a legalistic tradition, knows that some areas of his or her Christian life leave something to be desired. But if "good Christians don't get a divorce," and I got a divorce, then I'm not a good Christian. Being crazy at the moment, I state it the worst possible way: I'm a *bad* Christian, and all the rejection, isolation, and disapproval I feel are punishment for my failure as a Christian. I don't even have the resources to help me find my faith again. Only if the spouse was blatantly, obviously "bad," does the church respond with sympathy for the "innocent" partner, but rarely are cases that clear-cut. Most often, we are left with a sense that we aren't Christian enough to have a legitimate need and right to call on God for help in this time of great trouble. In fact, we even get angry at God for "allowing" the divorce to happen. Many Christians are taught that God can do anything, and that when we pray properly God can work miracles. "But I did pray, and God didn't save the marriage, and that makes me angry." Whereupon my legalistic Christian conscience tells me that anger at God is blasphemous, so I have even more to feel guilty about. And so it multiplies. Sheer weight and number of problems, our church teachings and friends, our own consciences—all make it very easy to be and act "crazy."

This book will reflect some of the craziness inherent in a divorced Christian's thoughts and feeings. Though I am a professor, the book will not be scholarly. Because I am writing autobiographically about problems that overwhelmed me and overlapped each other, the ideas weren't easy to sort into neat categories or present with logical precision. Since I'm assuming you're as "crazy" as I was (am?) I don't think you'll mind if topics like guilt and loneliness and the ways our churches help or hinder us get repeated or talked about in different contexts. Everything keeps coming back to the chaotic, crazy notion of a "divorced Christian"—something that ought not be, yet is. And I want to tell it like it is. I have never written anything that was not filled with footnotes and technical jargon, but rational academic discourse and citation of sources won't help you or me. The book isn't for those who want theological explorations of the "divorce problem"; it is for those caught up in the craziness of divorce. Nor is it, strictly speaking, a psychological study. I am a psychologist and minister. This book, however, is by the person Lewis Rambo, not the professor, the psychologist, or the minister, though obviously those roles have an influence. I speak from my personal experience with the hope that my thoughts, feelings, and actions will explore some of your needs, and that we can bring healing to each other through the dialogue of this book. I invite your letters and comments.

Autobiography

Perhaps a brief account of who I am is in order, so you will know where I'm coming from. I grew up in Comanche, Texas. My mother was involved in the Church of Christ, and through her and my maternal relatives the church became very important to me. As early as I can remember, I wanted to be a Church of Christ minister. Religion wasn't important to my father, but he didn't interfere with my involvement or aspirations, and two maternal uncles who were ministers served as role models and inspirations to me.

The Church of Christ believes in the verbal inspiration of the Bible, and that the way to salvation is for people to study it intensely, discern the original church as revealed in the New Testament, and then reestablish that church with no human creeds, forms, or doctrines. The church tends to be legalistic, exclusivist, and evangelistic. Needless to say, one takes very seriously a form of religion that strongly emphasizes following the Bible very closely on such matters as the name of the church, forms of baptism, or the use of musical instruments, and whose evangelistic zeal is directed to winning people from denominations not equally strict. I rarely heard divorce discussed, and then it was vehemently denounced as sinful. Only in the case of adultery is biblical divorce possible: the "innocent" party was free to remarry, the "guilty" spouse was not allowed to remarry and almost certainly would leave the church. Lines of good and evil are so clearly drawn that there is little need for formal excommunication; whoever was "guilty" knew it and would leave voluntarily.

I became a Christian by being baptised in 1957 at the age of thirteen. From there, things went according to plan for someone dedicated to becoming a minister in the Church of Christ: college at the church-sponsored Abilene Christian College and marriage to a classmate just a few days after I graduated. Then came a year as a minister in Pennsylvania before I entered Yale Divinity School. I felt that these were exciting times. My work took my wife and me to places as far apart as Huntsville, Texas, and Wiesbaden, West Germany, and I have fond memories of a delightful summer traveling together in Europe in 1970.

But when I entered the University of Chicago Divinity School after graduating from Yale, our marital problems surfaced. My low self-esteem and the academic demands I was under made me frustrated and irritable and a very difficult person (I now realize) to live with. Also, my wife had had her own work as a high school English teacher for over five years, but she left that to have our daughter. Anna was born in March of 1974 and became the focus of her life, just as I was getting more and more involved in my doctoral studies, the pressure of part-time jobs, preaching on weekends to earn extra money, and so forth. I wasn't much help to her with the baby, and we grew further and further apart despite our best efforts at communication. I escaped into my work and my wife into the tasks of homemaker and mother. Rarely was there a meeting of minds or bodies for the enrichment of our marriage.

I can see now that I was too ambitious and self-centered to be a good husband to my former wife and too immature to be a good father to Anna. I found excitement and friends at work, and though I knew that all was not well, I didn't seem to know how to make life better for us, or even want to try. As my professional life flourished—I moved from a professorship at Trinity College in Illinois to one in California with the San Francisco Theological Seminary and the Graduate Theological Union in Berkeley—our personal life became sterile at best and hostile and strained at worst.

We tried counseling and other remedies, but finally separated in 1980 and were divorced in February, 1981. My ex-wife remarried later and moved to Mexico with her new husband and Anna. They now live in the United States.

Since the divorce, I've lived in a twilight zone filled with guilt, perplexity, excitement, and searching. Mostly, I've been looking for the "perfect woman" to heal the wounds of the divorce. I have dated a lot, and been involved with about five women seriously, with one for as long as ten months. Such a relationship put interest back in my life, and personal satisfaction, but I seem always to be in a limbo of ambivalence about having serious relationships: when I'm in one, I can't think of anything but getting out; when I don't have companionship and love, I'm searching for it desperately. But if this crazy, ambivalent attitude pervades my life, I have also been forced by the divorce and my reactions to it to analyze and clarify for myself how I've lived in the past and what I want for the future.

I see counterproductive, even destructive, patterns of action and thought, but they can be changed, and I also see hopeful options, new patterns I can make grow out of those which made my past less than what it should have been. I have some distance from the problems now, and that's important in order to find creative resolutions for one's life. It's a slow and painful process because it is, in part, a search for the fundamental causes of our divorce and my responsibilities in what happened to us. But such analysis can help me find better ways to living now and in the future, and it has led me to writing this book in order to share with others the pilgrimage of divorce and the discovery, through it, of new life and hope.

Wilderness and Promise

There is resurrection after the crucifixion of divorce: that is no Pollyanna prediction, but the genuine experience of many divorced Christians who have been willing to expand the horizons of their faith and to walk as pilgrims through dangerous, but sometimes delightful, territory. We're tempted to return to the past, to the old patterns, just to find peace. Understandably, we are not eager to die to the old life, much less to trust God enough to try new ways of relating to God and to other people. The path has hazards; there is danger. But if we trust God and are willing to join with other Christians, our pilgrimage can bring hope, excitement, and new birth. The pain involved is worth the effort because we find new outlooks on life in general and a new life of faith which has perhaps been weak for years or which we might even have rejected in the traumatic time of the divorce. We have to be honest and assertive setting out on this pilgrimage, and that is liberating though painful. It feels good to be candid, doing what you know is right, and so you are able to face your own needs and desires and work for their fulfillment.

At the center of the Christian's hope and excitement and newness lies our realization that there is *no* hope in legalism or in our own good works. We've shattered the old illusion that we are "good," that we are people who can't fail. Clearly, we have failed in one of the most important undertakings of our lives. But not because we weren't devout enough or good enough Christians: nobody is a good enough Christian. We're not being punished for this reason, and it isn't why we are divorced. The Christian should get it straight that being a Christian doesn't protect one from the problems of life. We can work to improve our life of faith, but first we have to realize that the gospel is for the failures, the outcasts, the rebels, the lonely, the brokenhearted. Having really heard this good news, we can stop wallowing in neurotic self-incrimination and self-denunciation and begin our journey toward a new life.

CHAPTER II

HEALING THE WOUNDS

For everything there is a season, and a time for every matter under heaven:
a time to break down . . . a time to weep . . . a time to mourn . . .
a time to refrain from embracing . . . a time to lose . . . a time to
cast away . . . a time to rend . . . a time to hate . . . a time for war
. . .

The Labyrinth of Guilt

Guilt has to head the list of difficult emotional problems that seem to surround us from outside and echo from within as we begin to recognize ourselves as divorced, or divorcing, Christians. In fact, guilt will appear again and again throughout this section in which I talk about the concatenation of feelings and responses that I, being divorced, have had to confront, and that I imagine will reflect much of your experience as well. (The best one-volume study of guilt is Edward V. Stein's *Guilt: Theory and Therapy* [Philadelphia: Westminster Press, 1968]. For an excellent discussion of the topic that is geared to a less academic audience, see Edward V. Stein's *Beyond Guilt* [Philadelphia: Fortress, 1972].)

Naturally everybody feels guilt during divorce, but as Christians we have to bear not only the failure and family pressures of the divorce, but also a strong sense that we've violated the strictures of the church and even of God. We may become suicidal with the hopeless feeling of having disobeyed God's will: I've done this horrible thing, and there is no way to atone for the sins of the past; I'm miserably alone now, rejected by the church and my friends, and I'm damned for eternity because of my crime. If that sounds overstated to some of you, others from legalistic traditions, will know the agony of a ruthless conscience that haunts us every step of the way, and even invades our dreams to disrupt the fleeting moments of escape and refreshment sleep should bring. So it is essential for us to make an important distinction at the outset: the difference between real guilt and neurotic guilt. Ironically, real guilt is more easily dealt with and forgiven, whereas neurotic guilt is a more pernicious, destructive force.

Neurotic guilt is a form of self-destruction and self-rejection that leads us constantly to condemn ourselves for being such horrible, unlovable people. We can list our wrongdoings endlessly, both the significant and the trivial ones. But our sense of internal balance is missing, and in the heat of the crisis we can't find more objective, rational ways of viewing ourselves and the mess we're in. Neurotic guilt doesn't listen to reason or balanced objectivity: the savage taskmaster is at work in us, seeking to humiliate and destroy us. "If only I had done this or that or the other," we hear ourselves repeating to ourselves, "the divorce wouldn't have happened." Well, that may be true. But the divorce did happen, and our job now is to learn from it rather than to engage ourselves in endless self-mutilating battles of self-hatred.

Of course, we are often too "nice" to be willing to face the rage we feel at our situation, or the hostility we have for our former spouse. We have those feelings, however, so we have to do something with them. And often it's easier to direct them at ourselves than to recognize the murderous anger we feel toward the one who rejected us, toward the spouse's lover, or toward the other real objects of our rage, whoever they might be. So we feed the fires of guilt, unconsciously diverting hostility from others to ourselves. This is where other divorced Christians come in. If you can meet and talk together frankly with other people in your same situation you'll discover that Christians just as "nice" as you are can be as angry and consumed with hostility as you. And talking frankly with one another, you'll be able to face the feelings and work through them. I am not recommending wallowing in the feelings; the idea isn't to express them in order to nurture them. But unless we face the rage and hostility directly, and work through them productively, we will continue to carry the burdens of anger and neurotic guilt into new relationships, into a state of general malaise, or even into psychosomatic disorders. Honesty about feelings can become the means to taking a major step forward in healing the wounds of divorce.

The response to divorce, the kind or degree of guilt we feel, may well be determined by whether we were rejected or did the rejecting. Divorce has its "rejectees" and its "rejecters." (While some divorces may seem to come about by mutual agreement, one spouse in such a "congenial" divorce was probably more interested in obtaining it than the other.) The rejecter might seem to be better off emotionally at first, feeling elated at being finally free of a desperate situation. I've even heard a few women say that their divorce meant they now had only two children to care for instead of three, and men no doubt have similar ways to put down a wife they've rejected.

So at first the rejected spouse has the hardest problem. You feel your husband or wife repudiated you and your best efforts. You're helpless to do anything to reclaim the situation; you're dejected and raging inside because the key person in your life left you for someone else, or hurting deeply because you have turned out to be just so generally unpleasant that your spouse would leave you for nobody at all. If there were a lover, then you've been betrayed. But if you were in a "bad relationship" and your wife or husband simply wanted to get away from you, you can feel even worse because there isn't any other person or thing to see as having come between you; "betrayal" is at least clear-cut—this is just impossible to understand. Rejection, whatever its cause, leaves you reeling with internal pain.

But the one who does the rejecting may find after a while that elation gives way to remorse for having broken up the marriage. Perhaps you were in a situation so horrible that you feel safer and have more peace of mind outside of marriage. Certainly nobody would blame you for such feelings of relief if you had been living with an alcoholic or physically abusive, or merely grossly irresponsible, spouse. Nobody, but you: "Surely I could have done something to 'save' the marriage or change my husband or wife for the better; if only I'd been stronger I could have tolerated the situation longer and been a better influence; I've 'failed' or maybe I was just stupid for having married that person in the first place." These and other such thoughts could displace the relief with guilt. Even if you rejected someone you had simply grown to feel was incompatible, you'll probably become guilty over seeing the pain you've given someone you used to love. That raises the interesting and typically crazy problem caused when rejectees make their suffering obvious to the rejecters in order to make them feel guilty. I, at least, tried to make my former wife so aware of my pain that she would suffer from seeing the terrible things she'd done to me (she was wise enough not to fall into that particular neurotic trap I had attempted to set). Such a strategy is not usually conscious, but it often works.

Guilt, though involved in all these responses, is not a constructive emotion for either spouse. We end up generating bad feelings in ourselves and in each other without producing either a little self-esteem for our wounded egos or, certainly, a prospect of reconciliation. Guilt only forces us to look for more justifications for the break-up of the marriage.

Who's to Blame?

The mirror image of guilt is blame, and for some Christians who divorce, blame is both a personal response and a church issue. This book isn't concerned with theological technicalities, but the pernicious practice in legalistic church circles of establishing blame in the divorce has bearings on our internal process and progress. The need to call one person "guilty" and the other "innocent" is supposedly based upon the teachings of Jesus about the proper grounds for divorce. Here I want to examine the problems generated by this practice. Traditionally, the guilty party is the one who violated the marriage covenant by having sexual intercourse outside the marriage. Adultery is thus the "cause" of divorce, and the adulterer is the enemy of marriage. The innocent party has been sexually faithful and is free to remarry. It sounds simple, as most legalisms do, but the people involved get caught in a maze of problems generated by this mode of viewing divorce.

In the first place, those who are honest will recognize that only rarely is one spouse clearly guilty and the other absolutely innocent. It may be true that one committed adultery and the other was sexually faithful, but the "innocent" spouse may have appeared so cold, critical, and rejecting that the "guilty" party felt forced to seek love and affirmation outside the marriage. I think we can all recognize how often this typically human situation arises. I don't even doubt that at times the "guilty" spouse commits adultery in order to escape an unhappy marriage: knowing the wife or husband to be more strictly religious, and in need of a "legitimate" out, the adulterous spouse gives the other a gift of a free conscience and lets her or him escape, smelling like a rose. But if that sounds unlikely, what about those times when both partners have been unfaithful? Are both unable to remarry within the church's rules? Do we look at the clock or a tally sheet: is the first person to have committed adultery the guilty one and the other innocent, or is the guilty party the one who had the largest number of sexual encounters? This puts the supposedly biblical and religious issue in a ridiculous light, but it reflects precisely the sorts of problems that arise from some churches' legalistic mentalities.

In fact, we must recognize that adultery, whether of one spouse or both, is a symptom of their marital problems, not the cause of the divorce. Our churches have to face and deal with that fact realistically.

If nobody has been unfaithful, nobody can be labeled "guilty" or "innocent." Life simply has become unbearable for husband and wife, the marriage is dissolved, and then what? Remarriage? Some churches will grudgingly allow for divorce when there has been alcoholism, drug addiction, or physical abuse, but will then demand that the parties—even the "innocent" party—never remarry because no biblical basis can be found for the divorce. When life-spans were short, or when extended families gave a divorced man or woman somewhere to find affection and fellowship, perhaps such a solution seemed realistic or humane. But in our modern world, there are few options to a life of solitude for the single Christian caught in one of the many no-win traps of divorce. To rub salt into the wound, we find married Christians, who are sometimes in bad marriages themselves and secretly want out, urging their divorced friends to enjoy their solitude and not to worry. That, surely, is no solution.

The church's inclination to fix blame legalisticaly or publicly exacerbates our own internal process of recovery, for we ourselves want to be able to put "blame" for the divorce firmly on someone or something. Commonly, you begin by blaming your ex-spouse, especially if you are the "innocent" or rejected partner. Then you begin to shift the blame to yourself as you see more clearly your part in the break-up, even if you weren't the one to have an affair, or ask for the divorce. Here, blame and guilt come together: I'm a terrible person; I alienated my spouse; I caused it all; if I'd been a different person my husband or wife wouldn't have left me; and so on. During a third phase, you fluctuate between a sense of guilt and full responsibility and one of your spouse's having been wholly at fault. In the fourth phase, guilt and blame begin to balance out rather than merely seesaw back and forth: you begin seeing all the grey areas and fuzzy lines that make simple labeling impossible. And at last, you can begin to transcend the need for either guilt or blame, and to be able to forgive yourself and your former spouse.

The Healing Power of Forgiveness

Healing is slow, but we need the resolution forgiveness brings to ensure we don't develop abcesses, wounds festering inside us which will disrupt future relationships and rob us of possible joy. "Nice" Christians want to rush the last phase and hurdle right away into forgiveness because they're uncomfortable with the fluctuations of feelings and don't like being unhappy. But there's no fast way to get through all of them. We shouldn't impose our healing pace on others; I've learned the hard way that a little friendly ignoring is in order when loved ones start telling you, "But it's been *three months!*"

Or even, "But it's been *two years!*" You are not going to "live happily ever after," because a terrible crisis like divorce leaves scars. Months and years after, you will have times of second thoughts, sharp feelings of nostalgia, pangs of guilt. That's normal. You can't have loved someone and spent many years together without any effect; in one way or another you and your ex-spouse are part of each other. The longer you were married and the more deeply you were in love, the more sharp and real these feelings of relatedness will be. Why not acknowledge them, be grateful for the good memories and forgiving for the bad ones, and, above all, be grateful to God for the grace God freely gives you to feel forgiven and to forgive?

I'm not talking about any forced "happiness" that compels us to shout "Praise the Lord!" from between clenched teeth. We can surrender our lives to God, sense God at work in us helping us grow, while recognizing that maturation is sometimes necessarily slow; after this kind of surrender and growth comes a gentle sense of peace. Tragedy and joy intermingle in life, and God's kindness is at work even when we rebel or simply want to give up. "Nothing can separate us from the love of God." Not even our own bitterness or resentfulness, which may linger far longer than we think it should. It's never too late to allow God to heal your hurts and to forgive you and those who may have hurt you.

Forgiveness can be one of the most powerful forces to help bring the process of divorce to completion, if the Christian is open to expanding and enriching his or her faith. The first step to forgiveness is to forgive the former spouse, but that's easier said than done. I am nor urging you to make glib assertions of forgiveness or to deny your feelings of rage, jealousy, or desire for revenge. Real forgiveness of another hurts; and it comes after, never before, you acknowledge the other pains that brought on the unkind actions and words you have to forgive. You could make some kind of vague decision to forgive, but authentic forgiveness from the inner you won't find expression in a shallow, ritualistic utterance.

Genuine forgiveness grows out of a sense of one's own sinfulness and recognition that the behavior, attitudes, and feelings of both husband and wife were in some intricate way intertwined. The things you are seeking to forgive are, in some sense, your fault as well. Action and reaction between two married people are like a complex dance: you may well have triggered or stimulated your spouses' "sins" by something you said or did or merely are. So both of you had complicity in each other's deeds. Furthermore, genuine compassion is a prerequisite for forgiveness in that you will, by the grace of God, come to see that your former mate was as vulnerable and fragile as you. Compassion and forgiveness go together. You see yourself and your former spouse in the same light, learn to love and then to forgive both: I, at least, certainly had to learn to forgive myself before I could begin to forgive my wife.

Fickle and Fearful Emotions

All this guilt, rage, need to blame, and trying to feel one's way toward forgiving join forces to produce some symptoms most of us are afraid of because they make us think we are in fact going crazy. Most men, for example, are not used to weeping uncontrollably. In general, women are more free to express their emotions, both positive and negative. But a divorced man feels humiliated and afraid of outright insanity when he finds himself weeping at unusual times and in unexpected places. As time goes on, we may have fewer and fewer such outbursts, but all of us—women and men—will find ourselves crying at times for no apparent reason. And what could be more normal? The sadness of divorce, with all the rage and rejection we've been talking about, creates a huge wellspring of tears that must be shed. Life will be simpler if we can simply accept them and allow them to flow freely when they come. You don't accomplish anything by trying to keep a stiff upper lip. You aren't going crazy; something has died, and you are grieving. You mourn the loss of a loved one as you learn to live with divorce—and of an entire relationship, a home, perhaps your children, and certainly many dreams. It is natural and therapeutic for you to weep at such a time.

Suicidal fantasies also beset us, especially during the early months when despair and pain make thoughts of ending it all almost a relief. The pain would be over, the problems gone, the loneliness snuffed out. Most Christians may find it fairly easy to put aside thoughts of actively killing ourselves, since self-murder is a grievous sin. But without being aware of it, we can engage in fantasies of passive suicide—how much easier it would all be if I had a fatal heart attack, if the airplane crashed, if the car went off the road (and nobody else got hurt) . . . Such a catastrophic event, since it would wipe out our troubles, becomes acceptable, even "legitimate"; it would be "forced" on us and not really our moral responsibility. We can't think very far ahead anyway, and the future seems to hold only anguish. Death is a better alternative.

For the legalistic Christian, however, death does not stop suffering. After all, hell awaits the sinner, and "I'm being punished already for the terrible crime of divorce. But maybe if something awful happened to me, then God would consider the account balanced." Death and hell both terrorize and allure us. Some Christians with particularly ruthless consciences escape into either super-piety or the suffering martyr's role to avoid the connection between themselves and the wish to have it all end. Forced "happy Christian" countenances or long martyr's faces, however, sooner or later meet up with the real core of pain and anguish at the center of our being during this time. I don't have any easy answer to the problem of suicidal fantasies, but they seem—for me at least—to be part of the process of dealing with the past and trying to get on to a future that seems all too "impossible" at times.

Escaping the Present

In the time of transition, between what was and what will come, we are greatly tempted either to return to the past or rush into the future, skipping entirely over the present, trying to ignore its realities, even though they are what we are now. (I owe much to William Bridges' *Transitions* in this portion of the chapter.) This is understandable, since we are in pain and lonely and yearning for some form of peace that will give a little stability and serenity to life. But we can't rush to escape the period of chaos, confusion, and perplexity. The intense pain of the past is subsiding, and moments of real joy alternate with floods of desperate longing to get back to "normal" with a spouse and a three-bedroom house and all the accoutrements of the good life we want. Yet we need the present to get out of the past and into the future, so we need to make some use of it. We can use it to help us see.

Most of us see the past in one of three ways. Nostalgia gives some of us what we want to see: a wonderful, delightful past we'd give anything to have back. Of course, we don't remember accurately; we strip our former life, spouses, and selves of all their faults and only remember the good. This may allow for forgiveness and help us perceive those we loved without our present rage, but the fact is that the marriage is terminated, dead, and we can't gain anything by dwelling on the past. Or, as we've already seen, strict Christians typically envision the past with intense regret and guilt, listing their many crimes and playing the "if only" game: if only I could live my life over I wouldn't do this, that, or the other. We can't live the past over, and in most cases we would have to admit that we did the best we could at the time. That, at least, is a realistic look at ourselves and the past.

In looking at the past, the best use of the transitional period is self-examination: what can I learn from it all? We aren't to engage in endless self-condemnation, but we have to face real faults courageously and analyze real strengths so we can call them up again. Alcoholics Anonymous tells us that confession of past faults requires some guidance because the addictive personality typically exaggerates. We within the moralistic Christian milieu know all about seeing more faults than there are! But also, it's important to go beyond the mere enumeration of particular sins to look at the patterns of our lives which need to be restructured. Can I learn something constructive for myself, my children, and my future spouse? What did I do and feel and think that made certain ways of acting helpful or harmful to my life and to the lives of those around me?

This is a good place for me to use myself as an example. I now realize that I was a perfectionist. I was harsh and critical of myself for my faults, and my wife and child fared no better in my perception. Nothing was ever good enough. I had a vision of a perfect self and perfect marriage and perfect child, against which I could ruthlessly place all our faults, dwelling on them *ad infinitum* and *ad nauseam*. Perfectionism is a terrible disease common among some religious people; the legalism and harsh religious ethos foster a life-style that is equally critical, harsh, and vindictive. We can sound pretty angry and irritable about everything instead of encouraging each other, with love and affirmation, to go out into the world to live strong, creative lives. We dwell on our fears of doing something wrong, confirming our picture of ourselves as terrible, incompetent people. This is just an example of one pattern of thought and behavior that I can now discern with some objectivity. We can all learn to find these patterns, and to change and grow into more productive, affirmative modes of living.

Another temptation during the time of transition is to rush into the future. Everything will be joyful and wonderful, a great golden age. As I've said, that leaves out *now*: such romanticizing means the present can't live up to the expectations of a perfect future one way or another (unlike those of the past, from which we can learn), we're trapped in a vision that makes "now" only a time of fear and anxiety. But we could also learn to plan and hope for the future, without simplistic views of it as either a bed of roses or a terrible nightmare. It will, after all, be filled with the same ups and downs as the present, and we do find enough joy and peace in an ordinary day to sustain us. Trials and victories make life exciting.

We can all help one another find options for the future. Singles groups help people examine realistic goals for the members, based on age, sex, social status, health, children, money, and many other things. Most important of all, we need to respect and love ourselves enough to be able to face possibilities and problems alike with realism and hope. Some problems we learn to live with, like the paralysis of our feelings and ideas which prevents our making constructive changes. We have to face the inertia that makes everyone prefer to hold on to pain that is comfortable because we know what to expect, rather than reach out for new avenues of life that might, perhaps, hold pain also if we dare take the risk of launching out toward new horizons.

Simply put, we have three possible ways to deal with past, present, and future. With fantasy, we have either a glorious vision of wonderful things or an apocalyptic vision of doom and gloom. Or we indulge in an inner turmoil of destructive guilt and fear and hate. As we have seen, these are valid feelings at times, but when they become a way of life, the destructive emotions imprison us so we can't make progress. The third way is that of realistic hope. With the courage of faith, we can look at the possibility of the future and the events of the past clearly, not blinded by false self-images or distorted facades. So we use the present, live in it creatively, and prepare for a constructive future.

Risky Transitions

"But what do you mean," I hear you asking, "by 'live creatively'?" So let's look at an issue we all have to deal with in this transitional phase of our lives: our sense of unrootedness, of lostness, of loneliness, and our need to cure those feelings with new relationships. Often the sensation takes the form of vague feelings of not knowing what to do or what to say or what to be.

You're adrift in life, and that's normal. But you should stay alert and be aware of the phenomenon, because it's telling you of your opportunities to find new directions and to experiment.

Take the risk of discovering new friends, new interests, even a new vocation or a new direction that isn't as neat and orderly as the old patterns. Surely there are risks: you can hurt someone and you can be hurt. However, you have also been given what may be the most likely time in your life to shape it as you want. Money, time, and other practicalities may limit your opportunities to experiment, but they can't limit your courage in trying to see what possibilities lie ahead. You have been through one of the most difficult struggles anybody can face, and you haven't been defeated. You shouldn't be foolhardy, but you shouldn't be passive either: get out of the same old rut!

Dating, its possibilities and pitfalls, is a big topic I'll be treating later, but for now, it is useful because all of us want love and companionship to displace the loneliness, and dating can be a good opportunity to experiment. Most of us have an ideal image of the perfect person in our minds which prevents us from seeing people for who they really are. We eliminate an acquaintance from consideration because he or she doesn't fit this ideal image, and we may thereby miss out on a relationship that might be good and interesting and nurturing. The perfect person is a myth, of course.

For some of us the big goal is to find someone the exact opposite of our former spouse. That locks us into the old rut, too, because anything opposite is defined by the original model. For me it was and in some ways still is important to find someone who is more beautiful and more intelligent and more successful than my former wife. I'd feel worth a lot more if someone like that wanted me, and of course, if she's "better" than my former wife, all my pain and struggle will have been worthwhile. Such criteria aren't helpful and prevent our developing new relationships that *are* new—solidly based on friendship, love, and commitment between the person I am now and the people I meet now.

To a certain extent, we're desperate for affection and companionship, but it's best to see new acquaintances as possible friendships and not to be "on the make" for a husband or wife. Courage, which we need, doesn't mean rushing into things. We have to take it easy, to let relationships grow naturally instead of forcing them on a road toward the altar. Then we allow for growth in ourselves and the other person, letting ourselves appreciate each new friend for his or her unique qualities.

We need time to discover ourselves, so we don't need to become too quickly enmeshed in a new relationship. It takes maturity to experiment, strength to live with newness, and willingness to take risks and explore all kinds of relationships with new and different kinds of people. The time of experimentation can be one of great confusion and frustration. Most of us like some degree of order, security, and control in our lives; and when that is missing, we only get more anxious and frustrated. It's paradoxical but true that when you need a new relationship most, you are least likely to find one, or one that is creative. The less we are at peace with ourselves, the less likely we are to have constructive relationships with others. We even tend to get into relationships that feed the pathology of our current situation and make us more unhappy, more dependent, less able to grow in ourselves or with the other person. Emotionally needy people involved with emotionally needy people in the throes of divorce compound each other's problems. Serious relationships are delicate at best, so we must be aware of our own desires. Growing from weakness to strength takes time.

Forbidden Feelings

Feelings are part of the human makeup. We have to encounter, engage, and embrace them, whether they are "acceptable" ones of love and kindness, or emotions of rage, hostility, anger, lust, depression, or despair. Read the book of Psalms. There you will see the full range of human emotions expressed candidly, powerfully, even violently. But many Christian groups fear and try to repress feelings, especially those "bad," "non-Christian" ones. "Happy Christianity" is a curse to divorced people because inside themselves they know they aren't optimistic and happy at all, but are feeling many of the emotions not approved by the church. Our friends don't want us to be candid about such feelings and probably suspect that if we'd been "good" Christians in the first place we wouldn't be divorced, and there's something wrong with us now because we clearly aren't "healed" and "happy." In the Psalms, people moan and groan to God, and even shout at God.

The problem for us isn't human emotions, but the attempt to restrict Christian experience to a particular mode of living approved by a particular segment of American society. The old puritanical manner dictates that the stiff upper lip symbolizes the best way to live: self-control. But our emotions are clues to our state of being at certain moments and over the long haul. If we don't face them directly, we may face instead psychosomatic illness, distorted personal relationships, and other destructive facts of life.

One word of caution: as divorced people, we have to recognize that our emotional reserves have been depleted by the divorce, and that we tend to weather emotional difficulties less easily for the first couple of years afterwards. We need to face our emotions, but we may not need other people's heavy emotional problems—at least not yet. When we encounter emotional difficulties on the job or in relationships, we find them frankly draining. It may be you'll need to draw some boundaries to protect yourself for awhile; you might otherwise feel so needy and so prone to need to be needed that you get yourself helplessly mixed up with the complex emotional problems of friends. It is good to learn how to say no, and to withdraw when you need your own time to recoup.

A particularly difficult kind of problem we might face crops up when our own emotional signals get crossed with those of people near us. We find our own feelings in a friendship turning romantic, but the friend doesn't reciprocate. It's humiliating, because being "just" good friends makes you feel rejected, while the other person thinks it's something positive. If we're desperate enough for romance, we may wait for the friend to fall in love too, or even begin to play little tricks and make compromises so that the friend will see how nice we are. That won't work. The magic of personal chemistry which makes people fall in love isn't rational, and all the gestures of infatuation in the world won't change the feelings of someone who does, sincerely, want friendship rather than romance. We should either accept the friendship or withdraw if we feel too hurt by rejection. That requires knowledge of ourselves and our own limitations. You might feel guilty at withdrawing, but you will only hurt yourself and mislead your friend with your super-niceness. It's far better for relationships to be open and candid, not half-disguised by manipulative game-playing. You are fooling yourself if you think you can win someone over by tricks of kindness; romance doesn't work that way, and a little honest guilt is better than a lot of self-delusion. Life is too short for you to use or be used by others.

Dreams and sudden memories of the former spouse can bring on floods of feelings at unexpected times. Anniversaries of important events are difficult, and holidays can be very sad. However, there will also be times when, seemingly out of nowhere, a surge of nostalgia brought on by a sight, a smell, a tune on the radio, will trigger intense longing to be with your former spouse and to have everything "just the way it used to be." Be aware of such feelings.

You can't wipe them out by pretending they aren't there. If the memories are good ones, you can enjoy and relish them; if bad, you can try to learn from them. Facing emotions directly is healthy, because the alternative is repressing them, which doesn't get rid of them but only postpones dealing with them. It is impossible to put out of your life completely, immediately, or easily, somebody with whom you have shared years of living and loving. Some people will tell you not to dwell on the past—which is probably good advice—but you can deal with the past creatively not by repudiating it or pretending it didn't happen, but by searching out the meaning for you now. Vivid dreams about your spouse may mean that you're avoiding unresolved issues or that you're not being honest about the real feelings you have. As a good Christian, you might convince yourself that you feel hurt and rejected, for those are good martyrish feelings of suffering; but if you have a vivid dream of murdering your former spouse, your psyche might be saying you are really angry—furiously angry—and that you need to recognize and embrace your anger, because it's you.

Legalistic Christians can have a pretty hard time facing what the Jungians call the shadow side of our personalities. It's paradoxical that we have this difficulty, since we talk so much about the fallen nature of humanity and the power of evil. But the Christian world, or part of it, wants to see humanity as "nice" and Christians as exempt from evil just because they are Christians. So when we divorced Christians begin to face our emotions, we are terrified to see the potential for hate, revenge, and rage in us. This in turn can intensify our guilt and make us feel totally polluted and unworthy of the grace of God. The "shadow" side isn't pretty. The "monster" is let loose in the crisis of divorce, and we become petty, vindictive, jealous, even murderous and suicidal. And those aren't at all "nice" things to be.

In my own case, there was an incident in which my rage was suddenly uncontrollable. For several days I fantasized to set about killing my estranged wife, but then I realized that that would not be the best way to punish her. The best way to make her suffer would be for me to kill our child. Only when the full impact of that fantasy hit me did I realize the depth of my rage, the limit to which I had come.

What horror I felt that I would contemplate killing the most precious person in the world, and for revenge! Of course, guilt and remorse filled me, but facing this dark shadow within me made me realize my humanity, helped me see the hurt and anger inside which all my self-control and stoical handling of the situation had been hiding from myself.

Working out such rage can take some time. But discovering the potential for evil inside us can make empathy for others easier. You couldn't have had such an experience of yourself without thinking "there but for the grace of God go I" the next time you saw stories in the paper of people killing their children and spouses or going out and murdering strangers in their rage and frustration during or after divorce. It is, in fact, the grace of God and not our feeble positive thinking which redeems us and helps us open our eyes to see our human, potential ugliness, in order to become our potential goodness.

The hurt of divorce is terrible, so the reaction of rage, anger, and hostility has to be normal. Acknowledging the feelings is better than making them go underground. Seeing them may make us test our self-image as a "nice Christian," but burying them may mean they will ultimately surface in explosive rage, physical violence, or suicide. Suicide may be part of the whole depression syndrome common to divorced people. Some call depression "frozen rage," indicating the link between depression with its suicidal fantasies and the very normal rage within us brought up by the humiliation, hurt, and guilt of divorce. Christians might *think* they shouldn't feel these emotions because they should be different, better. But, theological considerations aside, we have them and have to face them. The grace of God is powerful enough to deal with our evil side. We can't eliminate negative emotions by denying them, nor can our churches and friends help us in our struggles by making us feel we ought not to have "bad feelings." We'll be talking in the next section about how we divorced Christians can help one another and how the church can aid our pilgrimage, but none of us will get anywhere until we have acknowledged the goodness and humanness of all the feelings we have in all the times God has given us.

CHAPTER III

MINISTERING TO THE DIVORCED

For everything there is a season, and a time for every matter under heaven:
a time to heal . . . a time to seek . . . a time to keep . . .

The issues I have been dealing with so far have been seen in a very human light, and this is fitting since I'm concerned in this book not with theological problems, but with the reality of divorce for Christians who go through it. Yet because we are Christians, our churches' attitudes toward us affect our experience deeply. Because we want to remain Christians, questions arise about the interaction between us and the church, whether that means our local congregations or the broader context of the Christian community. The individual needs to find ways to grow in faith during this difficult time, not to feel cast out or abandoned. So, whatever the theological problems surrounding divorce and remarriage, the church has to respond. Divorce is a fact of modern life; it affects people in every church in the United States. Any church that doesn't face this reality is avoiding the needs of its own congregation and neglecting a vast number of people in need of its ministry. The hurts suffered by divorced Christians leave them raw, desperate for the love, kindness, and forgiveness to be found in a community of people who love and worship the suffering servant Jesus Christ. I hope in these pages to look at a few of the ways our churches can minister to us during our pilgrimage and at some of our responsibilities as divorced Christians to the church and to each other.

Why Did God Let This Happen?

One abstract problem, however, deserves some airing before I get down to more practical issues. "How is it possible for an all-powerful and perfectly good God to allow suffering?" Theologians call their exploration of this question "theodicy," but for divorced Christians the abstraction takes on flesh and blood as they try to live through all the pain and disruption divorce has brought to their personal experience.

Maybe we have sincerely tried to be good Christians all our lives. Maybe we prayed long and hard for the healing of our marriage. Or maybe we were just left stunned by the discovery of an affair or by our spouse's inexplicably sudden departure. In any case, we begin to ask: How can God be letting this happen to me? Doesn't God care? How can God allow me to be left with all these debts, with the children, with all my other problems? Why doesn't God intervene to heal my spouse and me and our marriage? Why is God "failing" like this by not listening to all my prayer and supplication? Whether such questions arise because of the death of a loved one or from out of the tumult surrounding divorce, there aren't any easy answers, and most theological arguments sound pretty frail to us when we're facing real human suffering. For some Christians, the biggest problem is finding ourselves actually angry with God and God's apparent failure to "make things right," and with our possible resulting loss of faith. Since it is a basic issue for us as divorced Christians, I want to dwell on it for a moment, because we can't get help from our church if we let despair rob us of faith and so leave the church.

Paradox is one of the most accurate ways of doing or stating theology because it lets us talk about God in statements that resonate with truth for us but that aren't precisely rational (and God's work in the world certainly can't be limited to merely reasonable human terms). Two such terms for me are "ruthless grace" and "savage mercy." God's mercy is "ruthless" in that we sometimes feel as if God were saying to us: "I'm going to get you one way or another! I have become incarnate and lived with you in the flesh of Jesus. If you refuse him, I'll come to you in your friends and family. If that doesn't work, I'll come to you in someone who is suffering, oppressed, sick, retarded, insane. If even that doesn't work, I'll make you suffer tragedy yourself. Then you'll be forced to see through the illusions and mysteries of the world and of your own creation. Reality will force you to see my grace and mercy. You cannot escape!"

In a way, that's a kind of theology I hate. I don't really believe that God creates suffering in order to get our attention, to break our hearts so profoundly that we will at last listen. But there's some sense in which God's mercy is "savage." It is relentless, imaginative, cunning, patient, persevering, never-ending. Possibly it feels savage because we resist it so much, because we put on layers of armor to protect ourselves from God. We are blinded by the light and hide as much as possible. Like Peter, we say, "Depart from me because I am a sinner." God's mercy may also seem savage to us because we are too genteel for the realities that lie behind the doctrine of atonement: the Hebrew idea of sacrifice and the crucifixion of Jesus. But God works through such realities to reach us, more than through any of our more comfortable, insipid, and limp notions of the "love of God."

I don't believe that God orchestrates our suffering in order to teach us lessons. But God's power is so great that it can penetrate into all the nooks and crannies of the world, redeeming us through love that reaches to the center of all the muddles we get ourselves into. Our confusion in times of suffering is one of the great overall consequences of human sinfulness; yet as we question in those times, we are most open to face reality. We have no choice in the matter.

The ordinary things in life which allure us so much—money, power, sex, status—mean nothing when we are faced with the death of a child, a terminal illness, the end of a marriage. We are on the razor's edge and don't like being there. We can resist or submit. Often we resist by pretending a too quick submission that isn't real, like prisoners in a concentration camp who fake submission only in order to get food or clothing. They know they're faking it, but it's the best solution to a bad situation. The captors know it's a fake submission, but go along until they can enforce genuine, absolute submission. This sounds ruthless, but so is life with its suffering. We fear God and want to escape God. We doubt God: if there's no God, there's nothing to have to escape. Or, we domesticate God, making God in our image and keeping God at bay. Either way, God serves our purposes. But in time of suffering, we can't keep God away or reshape God to what we want: our defenses are down and God gets to us. God is supreme and not we ourselves.

It may be helpful, if you are wrestling with God and questioning the reality of grace and love in your life, to let your mind play with such ideas and feelings as these. If they do not "answer" the anger you feel for a God who "lets this happen to me," they may help you remain open to answers of hope and increased faith that God may provide. (For an excellent discussion of these issues, see *When Bad Things Happen to Good People* [New York: Schocken, 1981] by Harold S. Kushner.)

The Church's Role

The church community can help divorced Christians make of their suffering a transforming rather than a devastating experience. Other factors will of course affect the outcome for different people: personality, economic resources, spiritual values, our families' and childrens' responses. But our church is important to us, and if we can try to stick with God through divorce, we should at least be able to hope that our Christian friends will try to stick with us.

Unfortunately, many churches do not know what to do about divorced or divorcing members; they seem to want the problem to go away, and—we may feel—want us just to go away as well. A congregation that coldly ignores the divorce itself and the people going through it isn't much better than one that actively condemns, isolates, or in other ways punishes the divorced. But churches oriented to the compasson and forgiveness of the God they worship can provide a context of understanding in which a terrible experience can be made into a redemptive one. The alert congregation reaches out actively to support and nurture those who are suffering. They don't tell us that divorce is evil and bad: we already know that in the core of our being. What we need is loving fellowship, with faith enough to allow us to express our doubts, rage, guilt, and all the rest of it. A loving community will allow, even encourage us, to experiment with new possibilities, and help us feel supported as people precious in the sight of God.

The church, of course, isn't totally responsible for what we make of our lives after divorce. Individuals may suffer from psychologically debilitating wounds that may leave them incapable of recovery. But the congregation can be alert to the needs of its people, especially when they require professional help. I think it is part of the role of a church to encourage the person who needs such help, even to assist in paying for the therapy. In this way, the Christian is encouraged to get whatever help is needed, and therapy becomes an adjunct of the ministry of the church. Too many people still have the outmoded view that therapy is only for the "crazy" or "broken" among us, but with the church's encouragement, they could be freed from such notions and enabled to seek needed help.

Confession and Forgiveness

There's more to the church's role, however, than assistance and support on the merely human level. It should make some difference that we are divorced *Christians*, not just divorced people. We are getting down to the problem of guilt and sin, and I'm not sure how to approach the topic without seeming to condemn. On the one hand, Christians who divorce are not evil in some special way, but fairly typical Americans caught up in a social phenomenon of epidemic proportions. We might be seen as victims of modern ideologies which foster self-centered ways of living that seem inevitably to destroy values like "home" and "family." On the other hand, we are also "victims" of our own sins, which have been accumulating over the years. It's sometimes easier to be glib about the personal sins or faults that lie back of our inability to sustain a marriage than to acknowledge that we have, in fact, failed in this or that or the other way. Liberal churches, particularly, tend to minimize the role of individual fault by saying that divorce is something that happens to good people as well as bad. But in moments of honesty, and even if our church isn't busy legalistically branding us "guilty," we come to recognize that there were things we did which led to the destruction of our marriage. And in those moments—which we need—it does no good to tell us that "it's no big deal," that our faults weren't the cause of the divorce. "Let the past go" or other such weak psychological nostrums are no help at all. Instead, it seems to me, the Christian context allows for vigorous honesty and gives us help in facing the sins that may genuinely, if only in part, lie back of the failure of our marriage. And divorce *is* a failure of sorts. For such failure, confession and forgiveness are better cures than rationalizations, which don't really heal the hurt and the guilt.

One reason I'm hesitant to discuss this issue is, of course, that the legalistic crowd may grab at the admission of sin, see it as justification for a "hard line" on divorce, and intensify rather than relieve guilt for those who have to resort to divorce. I believe, however, that the risk is worth taking because we are talking about the forgiveness of sins and guilt, not merely the magical removal of guilt. If therapy is the way to relieve the sorts of neurotic guilt I discussed in the last chapter, the way to relieve guilt—real guilt—is forgiveness.

Confession is important for the Christian. Wrongs need to be enumerated and—this is important—discussed with a trusted spiritual adviser. All of us, divorced or not, have sins we have to face. Confession lets us see the problems in our past and understand how we can take constructive steps to change our behavior, thoughts, or attitudes. Making a list of your wrongs will help you be detailed and realistic about yourself: it takes thought to be precise about sins, but you also stand a better chance of clearing the boards. Discussing your faults with a spiritual adviser will enable you to be totally honest with another human being, and it will prevent your falling into the trap of either exaggerating or minimizing the sins. The process isn't easy, but it beats living with old guilts and old self-destructive patterns of thought and action. Confession doesn't make you magically better; rather it lets you ventilate sins that may have been corroding inside and eating away at your relationships with others. It lets you find a sense of forgiveness and new beginning.

Confession is not a negative, morbid process, and I think it's a shame the Protestant churches have ignored it for centuries. The benefits far outweigh the possibilities for abuse. The divorced Christian needs radical measures in order to start fresh, to begin a new life. Spiritual housecleaning is a wonderful way to clear up some of the residual dust of the past that may haunt our life today and cloud our future. Too many Christians live without the sense that they can get rid of past sins: I have to atone my whole life long, to say nothing of eternity. Unfortunately, many Christians feel that confession to God is sufficient and confession to another human is somehow wrong. I would agree that we don't need a certified person who alone has the capacity to intervene for our forgiveness, but I believe the confessor plays an important role: I can confront my sins and present them to another person for guidance, evaluation, and forgiveness. Confession can also be done in a small group, but of course the healing power of confession presupposes trust in those to whom we confess, so absolute confidentiality is mandatory.

So, too, is our ability to be completely candid. To get at the root of the wrongs in ourselves that led to divorce, we need to be entirely open, and this means all of us, "innocent" and "guilty" parties alike. Leaving out the unlikely possibility that one spouse was perfect, each has sinned against the other, and both have to face reality with courage. We have courage because of the mercy and love of God. The forgiveness of God is assumed. We confess, knowing we will be forgiven, without fear of condemnation, because we accept the love of God in Christ. Otherwise, despair would overwhelm us.

Blame is Destructive

We have seen before some of the ways divorced Christians can be hurt by the legalistic pinning upon them of "guilty" or "innocent" labels. And the practice of assigning guilt in connection with adultery is destructive and counterproductive not only for the individual divorced Christian, but for the church community as well. Both parties contribute to the dissolution of a marriage, as professional counselors will attest (and here I do speak as one who has done marital counseling, not just as a divorced Christian). Churches shouldn't be engaged in the practice of assigning blame after the fact of divorce: it does no one any good to delve into someone's past in order to see if this or that person is a "safe" member of the church.

The church, we have to remember, is not a country club for the righteous, but an emergency room for the critically injured and a hospital for those with an apparently terminal case of sin. People in the church aren't pure and holy because of their own works. Holiness is a gift of God whose vast love includes the derelicts, rebels, and outcasts of society. Any church that doesn't invite all—even the divorced—is not a true church of Jesus Christ. The good news is the forgiveness of God in Christ, freely given to anyone who accepts it. Divorced Christians know, perhaps better than anyone, the reality of their own sinfulness and their inability to save themselves alone. So a church that burdens its people with legalistic attitudes not only intensifies their feelings of guilt and rejection, but works against its own mission as well. Yet many churches that accept divorced people into their folds may feel that—in order to make clear the church's stand against divorce on biblical principles—they must make such members prove "innocence" in the divorce, and may even prevent them from participating in public activities of the church, from teaching Sunday school, and so on.

Rather than minister to the needy, the church in fact forces them out, "guilty" and "innocent" alike (and which is which?). Some people leave the church when they get divorces because they find very few ministers or church members who are sympathetic to their plight. Also, the family orientation of many churches leaves divorced people feeling left out and isolated, if not actually banished from the life of the church. It is also true that divorced people, in their crazy emotional state, are ready to project lack of forgiveness onto church friends and leaders, so that the slightest problem will be interpreted as gross rejection.

To be what it ought to be, then, the church has to work hard finding a place for the divorced, to let them know they aren't just grudgingly "accepted." Certainly an outreach group, composed primarily of the divorced to minister to the divorced, would be a first step. We need to be assured of the church's concern and support, to know that there are other divorced people on call to help in the bad times when we feel rejected, suicidal, overwhelmed with guilt. Fellow Christians who have had our same experience can listen to us and offer acceptance and support. In the early days especially, we don't want to hear platitudes about recovery from those we don't feel know what we're going through. The recently divorced are in no shape to hear shallow, easy words of hope. But we do need affirmation, affection, and, above all, a place to vent rage, to weep tears of sorrow and pain, to question God, even to wallow in self-pity for a little while. These are part of the healing process, which takes a long time and which requires the patience of friends, family, and church.

A Mission of Compassion

Divorced people ministering to the divorced: this should be our special mission to the church, even as it has a mission to us. We may recall the loneliness we felt when there weren't other divorced Christians in our church to help us, so we know that even when it may be painful, we ought to be there to help our fellow Christian. We should work to form support groups, networks of people who can serve others in their time of difficulty. We should have the courage to talk candidly with one another about our experience and to do the best we can to help one another achieve some form of healing in the midst of anguish.

The best form of help we give is to be present to the other person. We don't have all the answers, and whatever helped us may not solve someone else's problem. But we can love and accept others and allow them to begin looking at their feelings, problems, and potential in a constructive way. We have to be healed enough ourselves to be able to tolerate the rage, despair, or suffering the other person is going through. We may say to ourselves that we can't stand to hear another story of pain, abandonment, and loss. So we have to be aware again of our limitations and know of someone else who may be strong enough to help at a time we are unable.

Indeed, that is why it is vital that whoever is ministering should be someone who has worked through most of the problems of his or her own divorce. The reason is simple: if you haven't sorted out your own life sufficiently, you won't be objective enough to hear and be able to help someone else. As in psychotherapy, "counter-transference" is possible—the problem that arises when a therapist who is not healthy tends to project his or her own problems onto the client, confuse the issues, cause endless complications, and make the task of healing tortuous or impossible. You yourself, for example, may still have a bad impression of all men or all women, and instead of helping others be more objective about their former spouses, you may add fuel to the unhealthy emotional fires burning in them. Rather than heal, you would be harming the vulnerable newly divorced. The church should follow the lead of Alcoholics Anonymous and urge the ministry group to assign as sponsors only those who have been divorced long enough to have some perspective. We needn't make rigid rules, but exercise wisdom in order to provide the best possible ministry to people in the throes of divorce.

If it all sounds too hard, remember that we are there not to save others, but to be with them in their loneliness and perplexity. We are only the avenues of healing that comes from God. We do not have the resources on our own, or we may feel overwhelmed with their pain, or grow weary of their problems—especially when they remind us of our own. But we can be there listening, seeking to understand, open to the spirit of God which brings mercy and healing. It's not up to us to force the healing or hurry it up. Here is the advantage of having groups, rather than simply an individual minister, to provide nurture and support for everyone. The healer needs to be healed; anyone constantly giving out to others will be depleted of energy and inspiration—not to mention time—very soon. No one person can help alone; we're all in it together, and we have to be able to call on one another for assistance when our own wells run dry.

Again a word of caution: the old notion that we should keep busy and help others may have some truth; sympathizing, feeling the other's pain might make your own seem to hurt less. But there are times when divorced Christians, like all Christians, need to be silent, to withdraw, meditate, and be open to God's healing in their inner selves. Don't allow overenthusiastic church leaders to force you into doing something you don't feel capable of. If you need time for yourself, take it: you might have been evading some important conflicts in your own life. If so, your sense of depletion and the need to get away with yourself and God for awhile might be a sign that you have drained yourself reaching out to others while you have been running away from a problem that demands that you turn inward to continue your own process of healing.

Vulnerability and Vision

We have a responsibility to the broader church, too, and we don't have to limit our mission myopically to others in our same situation. Through the trauma of our suffering, through our awareness of our failure, we are sensitive to the needs and sufferings of others. And we can share with others our experience of redemption in the midst of pain. Some more "normal" Christians than we might live neater, more orderly lives centered on their jobs, homes, and families. But we've been forced to take a different view of life: old patterns don't work, old assumed verities are questionable. With a searing sense of the pain of divorce comes a sensitivity to the suffering of other people. We can use that sensitivity to serve others. Knowing the reality of rejection, depression, and all the rest, we can reach out to others in pain—the starving children, the lonely alcoholic, the isolated widow, the suffering cancer patient, those who are deprived in any way who live around us. We know, in our innermost being, the blessed truth that the gospel is for all; and having been through our own desperation and rebelliousness, we know what it means that even such people can be saved. If the good news of Christ means anything, it means that we have now to extend our sense of grace and gratitude to others in need.

We've learned the hard way that suffering leads to salvation. Without glibness, we know from our own lives that resurrection follows crucifixion and the grave, that the Promised Land is only reached after a great deal of wandering in the desert. Perhaps for the first time, we really know the wonder and mystery of redemption that comes in the death, burial, and resurrection of Jesus Christ and can be grateful to God for the deliverance that comes through a suffering servant messiah. It's painful and dangerous to go from one razor's edge to another, to move from the threatening brink of personal suffering to that of pain experienced in service to others in danger. However, we are grateful to God for having delivered us, we're thankful to people who ministered to us in our need, and we have to be willing to take similar risks and reach out willingly to others on behalf of Christ.

Hope and Possibility

Self-knowledge isn't easy or necessarily pleasant, but we've been talking about its importance all along, the importance of knowing who we are and what to do in order to become who we should be. Barbara Tork, a participant at a conference of divorced Christians, summarized in a poignant way both the trauma and the hope we all have to feel:

I hate divorce. God hates divorce. But since my divorce I have been happier, more peaceful, freer than I have been for years. I didn't want it because I'm a Christian, but since it happened, I'm going to make the best of it and start to enjoy living for a change.

This wonderful comment contains the sense of outrage and hurt we know all too well, but it also points to the power of God to make our life better even in the face of such a shattering event as divorce. Notice it's not a lighthearted view of divorce: the pain is there, but combined with *possibility*. Hope and enthusiasm help this woman make sense of her experience, and it's sad that many Christians in her situation feel they must be miserable for the rest of their lives in order to pay for their sins. As we've seen, legalistic church frameworks and theological stress on the wrath and vengeance of God makes the sadder view much too prevalent. However, once we've been liberated to a more biblical image of God, we can know the freedom and joy made possible by the marvelous love of God for us in Christ.

In the next section, I'm going to be talking about a few practical points, a few of the things we can actually do as divorced Christians to help ourselves. But I want to place that undertaking in the context of this sense of who we are—people who know that we couldn't save ourselves. We've been forced through our divorces to discover that we'd lived our lives not in full accord with the will of God and that to such people as we are, brokenhearted and lost, Christ comes. Out of our failure we had a chance to learn that our own feeble works never were the way to salvation anyway. We might have felt humiliated to know ourselves that well, to have been robbed of the pretense that we ever could have been "good" enough. But maybe a little humiliation is worth it to be able to grasp the idea that salvation is the sheer grace of God and nothing else. We're blessed to know that, and probably for many of us the knowing wouldn't have come except through something as traumatic as divorce. Through the experience we can now see the nature of our past lives and the consequences of our actions, attitudes, and motives. With such knowledge, we can still "hate divorce." But we can also set about "living for a change."

CHAPTER IV

LIVING AGAIN

For everything there is a season, and a time for every matter under heaven:
a time to plant . . . a time to build up . . . a time to gather stones together . . . a time to sew . . .

If we use this time to seek to grow spiritually, we will be able to see more clearly possible ways of living better, more enjoyable lives. Of course, seeking first the kingdom of God is the prime task of every true Christian, but we've been forced to examine our priorities, and we don't have some of the illusions that others have for avoiding the important things. We are now forced to face up to the call of Christ, and we are challenged by the "ruthless grace" of God. When we know ourselves we come to realize the vast love of God for us, which then enables us to have mercy and forgiveness for others. We are forgiven and thus we can forgive, not through slick "positive thinking" or psychological gimmicks, but through the realization that God is majestic and mysterious and that, beyond our wildest imagination, God seeks us out at our most vulnerable times. Grace is no longer merely a theological concept, but a reality that permeates our entire life. This experience doesn't mean that there are not more "dark nights of the soul" in store for us, or that we will always be happy. We may not even have the energy sometimes to be grateful. We can only passively surrender and learn to be joyful in the midst of pain. But the experience does convince us that God is love and that through faith we can explore the heights and depths of life and death and always be close to God.

Knowing ourselves and God this way, we've grown up from "happy Christianity" to biblical religion. We know that we can bring a message of joy and redemption to the brokenhearted of the world. We must not sell out for a perversion of the faith that advocates thin positive thinking and optimism as substitutes for the powerful, realistic faith derived from the suffering servant Jesus Christ whose resurrection gives us hope. The Bible is based on reality—the reality of the human predicament and the reality of the power of God—not on some self-hypnotic tricks of consciousness which vaguely promise happiness. Genuine faith is open to God and the world so the person of faith sees the two coming together to effect the transformation of the world and of the individual. Faith works for the glory of God and not for our own comfort and gratification, although deep comfort and gratification are a consequence of faith if not its prerequisite. This is the realistic faith of the Bible which we have to mature enough to reach out and grasp.

To find a center of faith and its resulting serenity in God, we can try to learn new avenues of approach to God. A silent retreat is one way to learn to listen to God speaking to you in prayer, meditation, and Bible study. Go deep within yourself and find that God is there with you and for you. You will discover the exquisite resources of the Bible and prayer. Do not misunderstand. Spiritual disciplines will be extremely difficult at some times and boring at others. The difficulties will come when an issue you've been avoiding is forced upon your consciousness and you don't have any busywork to escape to. Boredom is also common in the spiritual life. We shouldn't feel guilty about that, but recognize that there are rhythms to spiritual life as there are rhythms in personal friendships or in satisfaction with our work. However, for us as single

Christians to find new life and a new depth to our spiritual life, we have to be open to the surprises of God and to be shaped and led by the Spirit of God.

This is dangerous and exciting territory. A solid, maturing spiritual life will give us mission and purpose and will help free us from the intense craving for a relationship with another person. Such a desire isn't bad, but it can become desperate, leading you into destructive relationships and to difficult problems. Finding some spiritual grounding in ourselves will prepare us for a good, solid relationship should that ever happen. And if it doesn't, we may be sad, but we won't be devastated: a rich life can still be ours. I don't want to be glib on this point. I haven't found a new permanent relationship, and there are times when I am desperately lonely and yearning for a new wife. But also, there are beginning to be more and more times when I am content to have a wide circle of friends, to spend my time reading and working, or merely being alone. My prayer life fluctuates from highs to lows: sometimes there's nothing to say. My point is that we must learn to live with certain things we may not like, but which may be the will of God for us at the time. This is hard to take; sometimes it would be nice if we could receive a news bulletin telling us what God has in mind when things don't turn out the way we want. I still question God about the whys of my life, I often don't feel God's forgiveness, and almost constantly I'm troubled that I cannot forgive myself for past events. Those painful times are getting less frequent and of shorter duration. For that I'm grateful.

I also find myself maturing when I realize that as a single person I am more alert to the needs of others, more aware of the community, and more concerned about world problems than I'd ever been before. It's clear that personal needs can be a distraction from certain broader Christian responsibilities. We may have to realize that God may want some of us to be emissaries to our churches with words about the suffering of the world, that God may need a corps of people who have flexible, mobile lives, making them available for service in the Kingdom. That is a fearful thought, because I would prefer the warmth of hearth and home, but maybe God wants me to be a servant in a different and wider world than the one I'm used to. I get anxious when such thoughts move into consciousness, but I begin to feel a tinge of excitement and, as faith grows, a sense that "all things work together for good to them that love the Lord."

Spiritual Guidance

Another way to grow in your spiritual life might be to find a mature spiritual director who will aid you in the necessary movement from neurotic guilt to real guilt and to genuine forgiveness. The notion of spiritual direction emerged within the Roman Catholic tradition and is most fully developed in the traditions of the Society of Jesus (Jesuits). A similar concept is the "sponsor" in Alcoholics Anonymous. In both cases an experienced person serves as guide for spiritual and psychological development. The director or sponsor isn't an intermediary between us and God, but merely helps give us some perspective on our life and provides suggestions for developing our own spiritual resources.

The spiritual director, sponsor, or counselor should talk with us and ask to hear our confession. This can be difficult, as I've said before. Perhaps we should try writing down all the things we've done that we feel are sinful. Then there's discussion of the problems: the director seeks to discern patterns or themes, and possibly to uncover sins that we've forgotten or didn't think of as sins. I did this with a friend who is a minister, and the experience, although difficult, was liberating. My friend was able to help me distinguish silly or trivial things from those that were obviously part of my neurotic guilt, as well as those which were genuinely sinful. As a symbolic gesture, we burned the list of sins and affirmed that they were forgiven by God in Christ and that life could now begin again. No magic was involved, but the experience made clear to me how much harder neurotic guilt can be to deal with than real guilt. Real guilt makes us face real problems and take responsibility for what was and is genuinely wrong in our lives, while neurotic guilt paralyzes us and wearies us as we go round and round in circles. I also saw the smoke screens neurotic guilt deploys which prevent us from facing real guilt. Confession of real guilt demands contrition and genuine reformation of our life, which neurotic guilt often helps us evade.

Repentance is another word for all these things, I would want to argue that genuine repentance and confession free us from sin and enable us to live a new life in Christ. This is one reason I'm so strongly against the view in some legalistic churches that only the "innocent" party in a divorce can remarry. Confession, repentance, and forgiveness give all involved the right to remarry. Some argue that the remarriage of adulterers is an act inherently involving continual sins in repeated acts of intercourse with a woman or man who is not the original and only spouse. But let's be logical. We do not apply this reasoning to any other form of sin. If someone commits murder, we can forgive the sin and allow a return to normal life after the payment of just civil penalties. We don't demand that an embezzler never work in business again, but that such a person not engage in unethical business activities. Likewise, if anyone repents and receives—as we believe—radical forgiveness, then we should not prevent even a forgiven adulterer from returning to the church and to a full life in the community. I believe that the radical grace of God should be recognized and allowed to heal people so that they can return to a congregation where they will be encouraged to grow spiritually. The church is a community of forgiveness and healing, not a jury to judge the guilt or innocence of anyone. We are all guilty and dependent upon the love and mercy of God for our salvation. Mercy should be extended to others as to us so we can all live new lives.

Inner Conversations

Among the hurtful, if almost unconscious, things we do to ourselves throughout life, but especially in the midst of severe problems, is to engage ourselves in destructive inner conversations. (See Roy W. Fairchild's *Finding Hope Again* [San Francisco: Harper, 1980]. In addition to his discussion of the inner conversation, the entire book is an outstanding study of depression and ways by which Christian faith can help in therapy of the depressed person.) Think for a moment what goes on inside your mind when you make a mistake. What do you say to yourself when you look in the mirror? What do you say to yourself in a moment of introspection, when no one else is around and you start "explaining" the mistake to an otherwise empty room? That is an inner conversation. Some people have a constant pernicious conversation going on, repeating ugly refrains: you're a terrible person; you're too fat; you're too clumsy; you are a sinner! One way to improve your life is to intervene in those conversations and to seek to modify them. For most people this takes time.

After you have spent years practicing the speeches (so that you may not even hear them anymore), it will take time to be alert to the pattern of your inner thoughts, to discern those that are destructive, and then to begin to work to change them. They seem so "natural." They are the "truth" about ourselves. Don't be deceived: you can't simply change your mind and refuse to say those things inside you. Most of us will find it easier and more effective to observe the inner conversation and gently say to ourselves, "There I go again, telling myself I'm a bad person," and then remember that new maturity is giving us new, more "objective," and even better views of who we are.

Seeking Professional Help

How do you decide if you need professional help as you struggle with the divorce and the process of pulling yourself out? I've already suggested that your church and friends may be aware of this need: listen to them. But there are several things you can ask yourself: How long have you been divorced? How long were you married? How old are you? This information gives a clue as to the extent of your difficulty. If you've been divorced for one year after having been married for fifteen, and you are still depressed and find that life is flat, then you are "normal." You need a long period of time to come to terms with the reality of the divorce, grieve its loss, divest yourself of the explosive rage that wells up constantly in the early phases for most people, and then emerges from time to time in the stages of resolution.

It's hard to make any precise definitions of "normal" and "abnormal" (especially since it's "normal" to be "crazy" at this time), but several clues helped me make a decision to seek therapy. Do I find that I'm going in circles on certain issues? In other words, are there times when the same old problem haunts me over and over again without any forward movement, any progress being made? That is when a therapist or counselor can help you to break out of a self-defeating cycle. Another clue is that you may find yourself constantly depressed. It's normal to be deeply sad and weep over the divorce. However, if the periods of deep depression and gloom don't seem to be getting shorter or less frequent, then you should seek out a therapist. Depression is often a symptom that the mind, body, and soul are paralyzed in a state of "frozen rage," or it can even mask suicidal urges that you aren't facing directly.

Another pattern that might alert you to the need for professional help is the endless repetition of romantic affairs or relationships that seem to start out "wonderful" and then suddenly become "terrible." It's clear you are hurting yourself and others, but you don't seem able to help yourself break out of the pattern. This common type of behavior should stimulate you to find help before you do yourself and others more harm. Another clue: are you isolating yourself from your normal social contacts, or going to the other extreme of frantic, hectic socializing? Neither is a helpful pattern because you won't be able to regain a sense of personhood through total isolation or through manic activity. A better life will demand a balance between comfortable solitude and socializing. If you find yourself in prolonged periods in which the general rhythm of your life is distorted, and you've escaped or attacked the world in which you live, then professional help is in order.

One problem deserves special attention. While it is true that suicidal fantasies are common preoccupations for divorced people, they should not be taken lightly. If the thoughts about suicide persist, you should get professional help. If your fantasies begin to take the form of very particular, detailed plans for the way you would kill yourself, then the problem is serious. If you devise a plan and begin working on the details over and over in your mind, beware! If you start to enact some of the plans, stop! Go immediately to a counselor and start working to relieve the pressure that stimulated such serious actions. If you purchase a gun, stash some pills, or do anything at all concrete, you are in serious trouble. Your life, even if you feel absolutely miserable, is precious and should not be wasted. A good therapist will help you work on the immediate problem of the suicidal fantasies and actions and will also help you discern the underlying motivation and issues you're facing. This means hard work, but a better life awaits you. As we've seen before, there are many motivations for suicide, but you won't be able to find the roots of your trouble by yourself. Don't waste time. Get help. Call a suicide prevention center if you have nobody immediately in mind as a long-term counselor; they can help now, and you will then have time to find an appropriate professional counselor to work on the deeper issues.

When you do decide that professional help is in order, you'll want to use care in selecting a therapist or counselor. The best place to begin is with your friends at church or in your family: people usually know or have heard about someone who's been helpful. Here, I'm just going to give some basic facts about the five types of therapists available and make some general observations about what to look for in a therapeutic relationship. The first type of professional is the psychiatrist, someone with an M.D. (doctor of medicine) degree. A psychiatrist is able to prescribe medications if your situation is so serious that you need to have tranquilizers or need to be hospitalized for a time; generally speaking, this is the most expensive type of therapy. A second type of counselor is the psychologist, who has a Ph.D. (doctor of philosophy) degree. This means that the person has studied psychology as an undergraduate, then done at least four years of study and research in graduate school. The clinical psychologist will have had a full year of clinical internship under supervision. A third type of therapist is the social worker, who has an M.S.W. (master's in social work) degree, given after completing a two-year graduate program. A fourth type is the pastoral psychologist, who has a bachelor's degree, a master of divinity degree (three years beyond college) and often a Ph.D. or some other form of professional doctorate. A pastoral counselor is a minister with graduate-school training in psychology, counseling, and related areas, who has been or is a minister of a church and also has worked in hospitals—both general and mental—or other institutions. A fifth category of therapist includes people with a masters degree in some area of psychology, counseling, education, sociology, or social work, who have worked in a supervised setting and passed the required examinations for certification in a particular state.

The bewildering array of options shouldn't confuse you. Basically, most therapists work on the assumption that they are there to provide total confidentiality so that you can express your thoughts and feelings in a completely honest manner. The therapist's goal is helping you discover your own needs and resources and helping you implement solutions to your difficulties. A good therapist won't impose his or her values on you, but of course, value commitments make a difference and it would be useful to question the therapist or whoever refers you about this. Ideally, someone with a Christian orientation would be the best therapist. However, finding a Christian doesn't guarantee you've found a quality therapist, or the best one for you. The most important thing to look for at first is whether the two of you have rapport. That's an elusive quality but of prime importance, and you should leave therapy if you feel that the therapist can't respond to you in a helpful manner. There will in fact be times in therapy when you feel that the counselor is "on your case," but they may well be the times when the best work is being done. So I don't mean that you should leave therapy when you simply feel uncomfortable. However, if you do not respect, trust, and feel comfortable with the therapist, there's little use in continuing. If, on the other hand, you find yourself "counselor hopping," then you have a serious problem being realistic about the foibles of other people, and you are afraid of working on the issues you find painful. Finally, remember you are paying for the therapy, and if progress isn't being made, stop.

Relating to Your Former Spouse

Dealing with your former spouse is necessary when children are involved. In the early months and years of the separation and divorce, this necessity can cause anguish. You might constantly hope for indications of a possible reconciliation, or you may need to express feelings of jealousy, anger, grief, or tenderness. Every meeting is loaded with feelings that invade your consciousness, taunt you with unfulfilled dreams, or persecute you with guilt for wrongs committed. However harsh the divorce, you'll still feel lingering tenderness and concern. These are perhaps the hardest emotions to deal with because expressions of kindness and affection, even when genuine, might be interpreted as mere ploys for a better financial settlement, or as an attempted seduction, or as a tactic to gain sympathy.

Divorce, as I've said before, is a no-win game. The interplay of emotions is complex within you, so between you and your former spouse the difficulties are multiplied, and you won't find any easy way to deal with them, no simple solutions. The first step is to acknowledge whatever feelings you are having, even if that only means seeing an emotional chaos inside you. That is the reality, and it should be faced. However, it's generally better to talk about these feelings with someone other than your former spouse—somebody who's a good friend, alert to your moods and feelings, and tolerant enough to let you express them and explore them. The last thing you need is to be told by yet another person that "you should not feel that way."

Parenting Issues

Children have been the great bond of our marriages, and dealing with them gives us some of our most painful problems. (My book does not deal with the issue of the effects of divorce on children. For the best resource for information on children and divorce see Judith S. Wallerstein and Joan Berlin Kelly's *Surviving the Breakup: How Children and Parents Cope with Divorce* [New York: Basic Books, 1980].) Again, there are no easy solutions. If you have custody (probably if you're the mother), you have the more difficult objective problems in terms of the daily tasks of raising the children on a limited budget, working out the complexities of schedules, and finding time for yourself. You also have added burdens because the other parent isn't there to provide some help with child care, especially if the former spouse has moved. You have some advantage in that you have the companionship of your children, but even this can be a problem if they're your only "society" and you don't find friends to fill your adult needs.

The absentee parent, usually the father, is faced with the more difficult emotional problem. You may find the separation from your children as painful, if not more so, than the separation from your former spouse. There is no relationship quite like the feeling of love and connection between a parent and child, and when that's broken, emotional repercussions are inevitable. The problem is compounded if you live at any great distance from the child. As an absentee parent, you don't get to see the child often and participate in all the small but significant events of growing up. You may find that you become, to a greater or smaller degree, irrelevant to your own child. The child has to get on with life, of course, and in later years may even come to resent visits to you as interruptions of normal routine. Parents and children who live great distances apart have to live with emotional ups and downs. During those rare times when you are together, you feel the pressure to establish a strong bond, but there's not much knowledge of each other on which to build it. Both parent and child might feel desperate to make a good impression and achieve a depth of feeling which is possible over a long period of time. On the other hand, the emotional down comes when you separate and know that another chance for closeness is a long time off.

If you're not emotionally mature yourself, you might find yourself trying to win affection from the child which you may not have from others. That places a terrible burden on your child. No child can provide what a former wife or husband gave to you, and there's no way the emotional needs of a parent can be filled by any youngster. It is unfair and destructive to the child to expect it. You must take responsibility for personal growth and emotional maturity so that the child isn't victimized. On the other hand, if you're involved in other adult relationships, you may make the child feel unneeded or unwanted. I can understand why the parents of children who live far away tend to wall their children off emotionally. If you feel deeply about your child, you live with a constant sense of loss, with constant loneliness.

However, children need both parents and they should feel your concern even if thousands of miles separate you from each other. You can help your child feel loved by means of simple things like cards and letters that express concern, by telephone calls or visits as often as possible. There aren't any magic solutions, but I think we as the parents have to endure the emotional ups and downs in order to maintain contact. You will feel that you are an intrusion, especially if your spouse has remarried. And you will cringe when you hear your child say "daddy" or "mommy" to the new spouse.

That isn't the child's fault or problem, but it's a pain you have to face and a situation you have to learn to deal with.

This section of practical if not always easy solutions to some of our problems as divorced people isn't meant to be exhaustive. You should make notes on other problems and other solutions as you encounter them. But it is meant to suggest a constructive outlook and an affirmative approach to dealing with our lives the way they are now, in the post-divorce world. I think I've been suggesting two things to look for in ourselves: a degree of maturity, or the courage to grow up; and a spirit of adventure, or the courage to reach out. The next question raised, about dating, is of course only a glimpse into a whole bag of questions, problems, and possible solutions which revolve around a basic fact of life, our sexuality. And it's to that difficult, if sometimes delightful, issue that we now turn our attention.

CHAPTER V

DEALING WITH SEXUALITY

For everything there is a season, and a time for every matter under heaven:
a time to laugh . . . a time to dance . . . a time to embrace . . . a time to love . . .

Our sexuality creates for us divorced Christians both practical problems and spiritual difficulties. On the one hand, we are sexual beings accustomed, through our married life, to having outlets for expression and satisfaction of our sexual needs. On the other hand, sex is taboo: a terrible, evil, "dirty" thing that we just don't talk about in our churches, that we're not even supposed to think about, and that all our lives we've heard there is only one way to handle—SELF-CONTROL! People not familiar with our moralistic ethos would find it hard to understand the agony and guilt (and exasperation) we associate with those two "conflicting" ideas, sex and self-control.

But many divorced Christians, if not most, engage in sexual activity. That's the fact and what do we do with it? How do we understand ourselves when we know that we need and do something our traditions and our well-trained consciences tell us is the Number One Sin? Our guilt about sexuality can be allowed to paralyze us so that we can't move on to new, better, more mature and enjoyable lives. Or we can try to understand our natural human sexuality in a biblical light and come to some kind of practical terms with it. I think the second is the healthier alternative, so I'm going to be discussing in this section some kinds of difficulties I've faced and I suppose you face too, some psychological and spiritual issues, and some things we don't like to talk about (lust) and things we absolutely never talk about (masturbation). I think we need to determine what we're looking for in sex and why we're looking for it in order to understand our old fears and guilts in terms of our new life and its new possibilities.

The basic conflict we have to deal with is that between a view of sex as in and of itself an evil, perverse thing (together with all the accompanying church strictures against sex outside of marriage) and one that recognizes our normal, God-given, human desires for closeness, touching, tenderness, affirmation, love. Our bodies and our sexual desires are God's gifts to us, not perverse, evil things. We've been taught to think of ourselves as "having" bodies, as if they are something foreign, to which our real selves, our souls, just happen to be attached. It's better to realize that we *are* our bodies; they are part of what God made in making us human. The first view makes self-control so important: we have to beat down and keep in order some ugly outer material shell that wants to make the "real" you sin. And when sex is a monster we have to control, of course we end up paradoxically thinking about it all the time: our preoccupation with it lets it begin to control us.

But the Bible teaches that sexuality is something beautiful, an aspect of human life that deserves special treatment and protection, a natural yearning for closeness and the giving and taking which is love. We aren't concerned, when we fulfill our sexual desires, merely with genital stimulation and orgasm. We human beings are seeking to fulfill something deeper, our urge for a mutual relationship with another in which each nurtures, cares for, and sustains the other. The most powerful way that urge is felt and satisfied comes through intimate sexual contact. But there are

69

other ways we can help ourselves realize our bodies as part of us, and I think it would be a good idea for our churches to encourage, rather than disdain, such creative alternatives as hugging, physical exercise, and dancing. We legalistic Christians have grown up learning that such "evil" practices only led to loss of self-control, i.e., to dirty sex. How much more responsive to God's creation would be the attitude that lets us enjoy our bodies, even in contact with others, without always having sexual gratification as our only possible goal.

Consider this attitude in terms of dating, whether you think back to adolescence or just about your present single state. You could, even if unconsciously, see yourself going out on a date as an "evil" person who only wants to have sex; and of course then your date is just somebody equally sinful and single-minded. You're both terrible people. But you could also see both of you as people seeking first affiliation with another, through which might then come affection and mutual affirmation. That's a more accurate perception of the world, of yourself, and of other people. It's also the psychologically and spiritually better, healthier view. You see yourself and your goals as worthy, and your actions are legitimate means to satisfying genuine needs. Beginning with a first date and then as a deeper relationship begins to grow, our desires for love and tenderness are given to us for the enjoyment of life, the creation of children and families, and ultimately for the glory of God, who made us.

Frantic Sexuality

We're concerned especially of course with possible views of sexuality as they affect divorced people. We've admitted that divorce itself, with all its inherent rejection, devastates our self-esteem. If we add to that shattered sense of self the misconception that we have something perverse and evil at the very heart of our being, it can become too much to bear. We want the intimacy now denied us; we need tremendously the sexual affirmation which could cure our desperate sense of rejection. We can't control the desires and feel as if we can't control our behavior; so admonitions to self-control, whether they come from within ourselves or from our friends, just don't help.

If you're the "rejectee," chances are good that you will try to come to terms with your own sexual desires, and with your sense of betrayal by a spouse who may have been unfaithful, by finding other sexual partners. If you're a man caught with a wounded "macho" self-image, your wife's unfaithfulness might conjure up some pretty primitive feelings of humiliation, which you'll quite possibly try to cure through compulsive sexual behavior aimed at proving your manhood. In any case, you get more guilt, not needed self-affirmation. Again, it's a no-win game. One common reaction, especially among men, is a pattern of frantic dating in quest of the "perfect woman" to cure the pain of rejection by a less-than-perfect spouse. You might begin to have the distorted idea that anyone will do, even prostitutes or somebody you find in a bar—anyone who can give your ego a little support. Your desperate search for intimacy and its rewards alternates with your sense of guilt and revulsion at your own behavior. You're in a counterproductive cycle of action and reaction that won't get you anywhere, and certainly won't get you "satisfaction," even of the most basic physical kind.

But our deep needs for love and acceptance won't be met, either, by admonitions to stop this "crazy" pattern of thought and actions. You can know in your heart that your friend is telling the truth, because your heart is doing its own telling. But reason, simply stated by another or invested with all your fear and loathing of yourself, won't help you at this point in your journey. Your desperation clouds reality. Yet it's imperative for us to have friends who will stick with us in such crazy times, and in spite of our strange behavior. People standing by us will make their love for us felt at last; their gentle comfort and quiet guidance can give us finally some firm ground on which to stand. We might not like to have to look back on this sort of frantic sexual activity, but when we are able to put it in perspective, we will be able to find stillness and life and hope after the whirlwind.

Lust and Love

Most of us divorced Christians want to get married again. Let's think about *why*, and in order to do that, let's think first about lust as opposed to love. It seems to me that legalistic Christians tend to define lust very broadly and love very narrowly. Our yearnings for physical closeness and intimacy aren't to be associated automatically with lust and so with evil and corruption. Appreciation of beauty, delight in physical closeness, the warmth we feel when we cherish and are cherished by another person: these are wonderful gifts of God. It isn't necessarily lust, but it's very common for it to be called lust.

A truer definition of lust would see it as any perversion of our natural desires for sexual intimacy and sexual passion, when those good and normal urges are turned in such a way as to let us *use* other people merely for our own gratification. Any distortion of sexual desire that leads to sexual activity without mutual consent is also "lust" (lack of mutual consent doesn't just mean rape, though of course rape is the obvious example; it may mean those subtle and demeaning tricks by which one person coerces the other, even the spouse, by demanding sex as "payment" for a gift or for the grocery money). Physical gratification (which can be a good thing) would also qualify as lust if it is more concerned with merely relieving sexual tension than with establishing mutual love, support, and tenderness. Another way to say all this is that lust dehumanizes the other person and makes sex merely biological and mechanical instead of an expression of union, commitment, and loyalty.

Yet our moralistic teachings have made us feel that the real distinction between lust and love is "when it's legal": married sex is legitimate and everything else is "lust." So conservative Christians are sorely tempted to get married in order to have legitimate sex. Didn't Paul say it was better to marry than burn? The implications of this attitude are serious. People rush into marriage after having convinced themselves they were in love, when in fact they were mainly interested in being able to have sex legitimately and therefore without guilt. I'm not imagining this for the sake of argument; it's a truth of my own experience and one which other Christians have substantiated. And it's a terrible mistake. Rarely if ever do marriages survive, much less thrive, when sex is the sole or main motive. But our churches can unfortunately allow and encourage us to rationalize our feelings and motivations when our basic human needs come up against the real or assumed strictures of religion.

So what about remarriage? (I seem to keep asking this question.) If our first marriages failed in part because of this rationale, it would be reasonable for us to be wary of repeating the mistake. Reasonable, but not likely. Many Christians remarry much too soon, before they have worked out the guilt and the problems of divorce, and one of the prime motives is to escape loneliness and find legitimate sex. I'd say it is better to have sex outside of marriage than to get married or remarried in order to have sex. I don't feel comfortable being an advocate for such a position, which is one clearly involving theological problems for most churches. But in view of the practical consequences, I think it's the wiser course. If you find marriage necessary just to turn "lust" magically into legitimate "love," you'd better seek out the guidance of a trusted friend, minister, or other therapist. We are trying to find more realistic, creative ways of living in this journey of ours, so this is a good place for us to stop and think about our real motives behind our interest in new relationships. We don't want second failed marriages just because they provide easy "legitimacy."

Autoeroticism

Masturbation causes much anguish in the Christian community. Many people masturbate, and often they feel a deep sense of sin for doing so. Some feel that they are failures because they are not able to control themselves, and some feel that there is an evil force within themselves that causes them much conflict and agony. A sensitive conscience often condemns the person for the practice and even for the desire. There is no single or simple solution to the problem. An outright encouragement of the practice is too glib, and a total condemnation is unbiblical. One of the most difficult aspects of masturbation is the issue of fantasy during the experience. Is thinking of intercourse during masturbation a way of "lusting after someone"? Well, it is hard to imagine masturbation without some fantasy. The nature of that fantasy may very well be the source of the person's sense of guilt about the matter.

A fundamental issue is the Christian's relationship to the body. It seems to me to be the case that the spirit-body conflict has haunted the Christian religion from the very beginning. Few have resolved the problem, and we are now the heirs of the difficulty. We cannot face the fact of our bodily existence, and somehow we feel that we must reject the body and its needs. On the other hand, there are those who are merely secular hedonists who advocate "do your own thing," and that is not the Christian alternative. This is a complex area, and I have no easy solutions to the problem of masturbation. There is no direct biblical proscription of the practice. However, some issues are closely related, and they cannot be dismissed easily.

Masturbation is the subject of much controversy in the broader Christian community. In some churches it's a topic for dead silence. Or possibly, for a few whispered warnings that scarcely mask revulsion. Millions of Christians masturbate, and do so with guilt and self-recrimination because they do not or cannot control themselves better.

It's not a bad idea at the outset to remind ourselves that self-love isn't a horrible, un-Christian thing. Most of us masturbate at one time or another in our lives, and as a matter of fact, some believe this can be a safe sexual outlet for the divorced Christian—certainly one not nearly so destructive as the frenetic search for sexual encounters I described earlier. Through masturbation one can express self-love, affirm sensuality as God-given, legitimate, and lovely, and learn something about oneself as a sexual being. Despite the condemnation implicit in the old wives' tales we hear about "what will happen to us," the Bible contains no strictures against masturbation, and of course takes sexuality for granted. So there really isn't any authority for our churches' traditional horror of the practice. The scriptural passages usually quoted actually deal with coitus interruptus and the resulting problem of infertility: in an agricultural society, and when infant mortality rates were very high, it was imperative to have as many children as possible to ensure a family's survival and economic stability. But, authoritative strictures or not, many of us have been taught to focus our guilt on sexuality in general, and on this particular manifestation especially. (For an excellent discussion of the topic of masturbation and an extensive bibliography, see James R. Johnson, "Toward a Biblical Approach to Masturbation," *Journal of Psychology and Theology*, 1982, 10, 137-46.)

If we think, instead of masturbation, in light of the real biblical understanding of love, which includes self-love, we may rid ourselves of guilt and think of its possible usefulness as well as possible abuse. Women may have experienced orgasm rarely in sexual intercourse, and masturbation can help them learn methods which bring fuller sexual gratification. Most of us fantasize, and since self-love (as Jesus' commandment makes clear) is involved in love of others, it may be helpful to focus your fantasies on the tender, nurturing, and constructive aspects of love-making rather than on violent, manipulative, or destructive ones. Fantasies of sexual passion and vitality aren't wrong, but unloving ones will, in the long run, produce more guilt through an immature sexual orientation. Likewise, if you simply let yourself descend more and more into an inner world isolated from community and friends, masturbation could help make all your problems worse. We want to remember the "merely biological and mechanical" quality of lust and that love involves us with others. Finally, any constant preoccupation with sexuality should alert us to ask what's missing in life and lead us to seek help getting things back in balance.

As with other questions we confront about ourselves, we can find help if we have a trusted support group in which we can candidly and honestly express our doubts, our feelings, our needs. On this particular topic, members of a group can help one another simply by letting everyone know that "I'm not the only sinner in church!" You'll find it refreshing to be able to laugh and talk with other normal people about things you've been so afraid and ashamed of that you've hardly ever even used the word. But candid discussion can help those who want to quit, too, as well as those who simply need to gain a more realistic picture of their own sexuality. We have to talk with one another to "demythologize" our human needs and actions. Some Christians will find this a difficult topic, needless to say, but silence or condemnation hasn't helped us know ourselves realistically. Shouldn't we seek out other Christians as we look for genuine Christian solutions to our desire for intimacy and love?

Searching for Intimacy

If you are reading this book, you're probably still unmarried and probably looking for new relationships, whether you've been divorced for a month or for several years. You've found that relationships in the new single world are fragile at best and volatile at worst. People like you who are available and looking are most likely scarred. We're in our late twenties, or our thirties and forties; we've seen relationships come and go, and we've been hurt but not always healed. We're ambivalent: we want a "meaningful relationship," but we're afraid of intimacy. We desperately want love, but are only minimally capable of trust. We beckon to others warmly with one hand, and stiff-arm them with the other. So look closely at the rest of us and notice that, like you, we're emotionally unstable or even disabled. Romantic relationships are primordial in that no feeling, thought, or action isn't in some way shaped by our past experience of love and rejection, of security and anxiety, which has given us our sense of worth and our place in the world.

Primordial, volatile, and fragile: but we want the new relationship. Love is blind, they say, and desperation makes us deaf and dumb also. We find ourselves madly in love with the most unlikely people, and possibly in bed too. So it might be worthwhile to realize some typical patterns people go through as they become sexually active after divorce. We've already touched on what for many is the "first phase," a time of frantic looking for a renewed sense of our own value in which we are, if not promiscuous, at least quite unselective about our sexual partners. And as we've seen, promiscuity only lowers our self-esteem without curing our rejection. Yet we may go on having casual sex for months or even years without realizing we're destroying ourselves. Maybe we don't even sense how much fuel we're stockpiling to feed our fires of Christian guilt.

If something—a friend or a book like this one or our own conscience—helps us regain some sense of self-worth, we might go into a phase of being very selective about sexual relationships. We're no longer desperate for affirmation, but we enjoy sex with somebody we really care about. Unfortunately, these "meaningful" relationships tend to go through about a three-month cycle. It seems many of us out there in the single world really want full commitment, but get cold feet after a three- or four-month dose of reality with someone. We might even try living together, only to discover we weren't as compatible as we had thought.

After several such relationships, we figure enough is enough. We put sexuality on a back burner and learn to develop deep friendships with people of both sexes. We've learned the hard way that romance is complicated and that living alone has its advantages. Perhaps through a spiritual director or through meditation and prayer, or just through our regained common sense, we get back a little peace of mind. We learn to center ourselves on the values and goals we find worthwhile. We become capable of living life alone or of waiting for the right person who will be both compatible and mature. The frantic and selective phases are over, and we're looking for a quality life, which we now know can be rich whether we live as single people in community with others or find a new spouse and all that deep sexual relatedness has to offer. Some of us choose the single life permanently; others are willing to be content—although sometimes lonely and unhappy—and to know we can enjoy beneficial lives even though we're single for now.

The very best of us in this phase become those whom Henri Nouwen calls the "wounded healers." They know that the price they've paid for wisdom is dear, but they know the love and mercy of God and are willing to submit their lives to God's purposes. They give their lives in service to church and community, and work becomes no longer a "job" but a vocation. People like this who have lived through divorce, experienced all the pain and growing we've been mulling over in this book, and still survive with a thriving faith—these are some of the most mature and graceful people you will ever meet. Their dignity and charm and compassion are gifts they give to the rest of us as they bring joy and healing into others' lives.

Dating for the recently divorced can be hilarious and horrendous and a hazard. Old, long-lost feelings from adolescence return. I have felt that my pimples were going to come back at any moment. I've known the intense fear of making that first telephone call to ask someone out for a date. I've suddenly become anxious about body odor, my clothes, or telltale dandruff—seemingly decades after these worries first plagued me in high school. Fortunately, out of fear or courage (I don't know which), I mentioned this to some of the women I dated early on, and we could laugh over it together because the same thing was happening to them.

For one thing, we're not really prepared for the dating game. The single world has changed dramatically while we've been married.

We are older without being necessarily wiser, and we're back on the battlefield in the war of the sexes feeling like toy soldiers. It's harrowing, but you can't do much about it except to have courage, take some risks, and see what happens. I myself found I didn't know popular culture as well as some of the women I dated, and I felt out of my element. The world I knew was church and academia, neither of them particularly rich sources for relaxed, nonthreatening social conversation. The rest of the world was a jungle to me, with modes of living I could hardly imagine and places like singles' bars where I didn't know how to act. Clearly, it would be well to develop your sense of humor.

A major problem for us newly divorced arises because we're so desperate that it's hard not to see every first date as leading to marriage. You can't be calm, relaxed, and merely yourself when you're trying to win people over so that you get some affirmation (and maybe a wife or husband!) in the process. You aren't lying, but you are trying to present yourself so that you fit your date's expectations; you're not really being who you are in yourself. You are simply not comfortable with yourself in this stage of your divorce or in this scary endeavor of dating, and you aren't in any condition to be truly someone of integrity. Perhaps the best policy would be not to date for six to twelve months. Of course, that's difficult, if not impossible. We need and want companionship and have to live with whatever damage we inflict on others and they on us. After an initial feeling that there's a world full of wonderful people out there just waiting for us, we discover the limitations of reality. Not only does the first date not end in marriage, but we don't even have the range of contacts we had expected. Reality is painful once again, and learning it takes time and energy.

Terror of Rejection

Rejection rears its ugly head as we set about trying to find dates and find out whether a date is going to lead to something more. The fact is that few people will be "turned on" romantically to you, so you'd better be prepared to be rejected. At least it feels like rejection, even when a date wants to affirm you as a friend but not as a sexual partner. You may know rationally that you shouldn't worry about this kind of acceptance, but reason doesn't help. You're at too vulnerable a point in your life, remembering not only the recent (and much more real) rejection by your spouse, but also long-forgotten but repressed feelings from childhood that "nobody likes me." Of course, people did like you, and they do now; it's just that they don't like *everything* about you, and you're in a pretty tender emotional state in which anything short of absolute, total acceptance feels like rejection. The pain is real, if irrational, and nothing you do or tell yourself will protect you from it at some point in the dating process. In fact, you're so vulnerable that this "insult" of proffered friendship-*sans*-romance seems to confirm your recent injuries: "My ex-spouse was right. I'm a terrible, unlovable person. My former spouse knew me better than anybody, and rejected me! Of course everybody else in the world is going to reject me too!"

There's also the other side of the coin; the time will come when you have to do the rejecting in order to be honest about yourself and with your date. You will be torn because you know what it feels like to have someone else be "frank" and "honest" when what you want is love. You know that we hurt people we like by telling them we're not interested in romance. But the alternative is that we continue to try to be "nice," and so end up leading others on when there is no realistic possibility of another kind of relationship. This dilemma is painful, one that's almost calculated to work into the guilt syndrome so popular among some Christians.

But it is imperative that you learn to be honest, to tell others what you think and feel about the possible future of a relationship. We do get early indications, from value commitments, physical appearance, personality styles, and so forth, as to whether someone is attractive to us or not. So if what you want with someone is friendship, it's important to make that clear. It's not only kind—to you and your date—but it preserves dignity and the possibility for continued friendship for both of you. If I sound terribly cool and rational on this subject, let me say that I've been on both ends of the stick several times, and it hasn't been easy. I hate to hear it and I hate to say it. It's almost as if I want to preserve the good feelings of the entire world, and I wouldn't be surprised if you recognize that very human desire in yourself. But we can't let relationships drag on waiting for something to happen that will relieve us of the burden of speaking and being ourselves. Endless ambivalence is cruel to us and to the other people involved.

Another twist in this knotty problem of "sex-and/or-friendship" comes about because, with divorce, we've lost our readily identifiable labels of "available" or "not available" among our own friends. Friendships that date from before our divorce can be stretched or broken because of this phenomenon. As married people we had protection from the acting out of furtive romantic and sexual longings. A married person is safe, and people leave us alone—for the most part. Complications emerge with divorce. An unmarried woman is now a threat to couples she's known for years. Everybody has some insecurities, so a wife suddenly develops jealousy for the newly divorced woman who—she's quite sure—is going to lead her husband astray. Or men discover they want to be "helpful" to the divorced woman by being solicitous or even by making passes or propositions that will restore her confidence. For his part, a divorced man can arouse jealousies with women friends, some of whom may have harbored hopes of romantic attachment from which he is no longer "safe." We suddenly find ourselves having to balance brutal honesty and tact. Somehow, we have to let kindness and integrity do all they can do, while knowing that we are ultimately responsible for our own actions and nothing more.

Filling the Void

Since we're talking about honesty, it would be well to think about our expectations in dating in relation to our thoughts and feelings about our former spouses. We often are looking to a new acquaintance to be either a replacement for, or an exact opposite of, the wife or husband we no longer have. In either case, as we've said before, we're trapped in the mold of the former relationship. There's no mystery here. It's a fact of life that we will, on the one hand, have a great deal in common with people who share some of the interests, commitments, and physical qualities of the former spouse with whom we spent part of our life. And on the other hand, we'll be wanting to get away from anything that reminds us of the person who has given us so much pain. We need to reach out and draw in to our lives new kinds of people and new kinds of relationships: that's the importance of experimenting. But we will also often want just to return "home" and find comfort in the sorts of people and activities that have given us comfort in the past. Both exploration of new views of ourselves and confirmation of the good that was in the old are important to our new life.

However, never, never, never tell a date, "You remind me so much of my former spouse!" That is the kiss of death. It may be a true statement, and one you mean as encouragement and affirmation. But it's calculated to turn away anyone else, who of course expects to be appreciated for his or her own uniqueness. We are each special, if only to ourselves. And whether your new acquaintance takes your statement as an insult or a very weak gesture of praise, you can be sure it will be taken in some way that bodes ill for the relationship.

In talking about the prospects and problems of dating, I've been sounding as if we are all going to set about the undertaking in a very rational manner. And in fact, I do encourage you to be self-critical in the process—which doesn't really mean we spend all our time analyzing ourselves: too much introspection, as I've suggested earlier, will give us worse psychosomatic symptoms than pimples or dandruff. But it is good to be aware of our feelings, to ask ourselves what it is about some people that makes us happy or uncomfortable with them. We haven't always been attuned to our feelings enough to have avoided mistakes. So now we simply want to be conscious of our own desires and expectations, to be able to sense what we want in the early phases of a relationship. We may not know all our requirements for the next relationship or for ones further down the line, but we'll have a realistic sense of ourselves which will leave us open to new possibilities and new discoveries of who we are and what we like. Our "requirements" shouldn't be unreasonable, but they should be clear.

Growing Toward Interdependence

Dating is full of challenges and humiliations which may alter and illuminate us, always (we hope) for the better. The ideal pattern to which we might aspire is one in which we—as a whole, mature individuals—seek out a new spouse in light of our own sense of strength and integrity. We're fallible human beings, of course, and rarely live up to an ideal. But we can try to avoid one of two extremes that could trap us always in immaturity. We can't be, or shouldn't want to be, totally independent or totally dependent. (The basic argument here is derived from an excellent article by William R. Rogers, "Dependence and counterdependency in psychoanalysis and religious faith." *Zygon*, 9 [3], 1974, 190-201.)

Total independence would seem to preclude any life with others, and yet some people try to have "relationships" while maintaining their own lack of any need for others. We become isolated even from the "significant other" in our lives, or merely interact with other people when it's convenient or fulfills our own personal needs. This kind of egocentrism effectively cuts love, at least as we've defined it, out of our lives because we only use people for our own benefit.

At the other extreme are those of us who don't feel ourselves to exist unless somebody else is there to give affirmation, identity, and purpose. You feel like a "zero" without another person—especially a romantic partner—to care for your emotional needs. Any relationship with such an overly dependent person is doomed to failure. Nobody can provide everything for any other human being. If you are the stronger, "dominant" partner, you'll either grow to resent the other person for taking so much out of you or to disdain yourself for being so locked into someone that you can't live your own life. If you're the "weaker," dependent partner, you will likely be jealous of anyone else who intrudes on your relationship, and you'll be constantly looking for signs of "rejection" (and probably finding ways to make your prophecies come true).

The ideal mode of interaction—which is also in this case a practical, possible objective—is through interdependence. Two mature people come together recognizing their strengths and weaknesses. You give generously of yourselves, yet have the courage to speak up candidly to express your feelings and needs. With honesty on both sides, little hostilities and irritations don't build up to explosive force. You can both be alone for periods of time, sure of your independent identities, but you can spend time together in exciting, productive living. You need each other not out of desperation, but out of respect and empathy. Your relationship doesn't block out the rest of the world, but invites outside friendships and activities because you know the two of you can't really be "everything" to each other. So the love for each other reaches out to include other people and commitments, which makes it a bigger love and gives you each happiness and maturity.

In any relationship, dependence, independence, and interdependence will dominate at various times as people and events change. During illness one partner will become more dependent. When one of you is consumed with a work project, you'll become independent for a time as you direct all your energy to work instead of to your partner. But the balance will adjust itself in a mature relationship; you'll establish a rhythm of give and take which willingly meets each person's changing needs, and you'll find and know each other in a loving interdependence that lets both of you grow.

Worrying, as we've been doing, about dating and sexuality and remarriage, implies that we are coming out of the gloomy past and assuming for ourselves a wonderful possibility: a future. I hope all our talk of growth and newness doesn't sound impossible to you, because it seems to me that growing up and reaching out really are possible for us, as long as we face ourselves honestly. I'm going to be talking about the future in the next section—not just about starting new things, but about building new lives and relationships. To do this, we have to see our past feelings and actions honestly and learn to trust feelings as important guides. Legalistic traditions sometimes portray feelings as fugitive and untrustworthy, when they weren't downright "improper." Some feelings are fickle, and we ought not to let them rule our lives. But there are others that come deep from inside us, that help us understand ourselves, and that we ought to respect. (There are several writers who have recently argued that there is a logic or pattern to emotions. See Williard Gaylin, *Feelings: Our Vital Signs* [New York: Harper & Row, 1979].) These feelings have a kind of logic or pattern to them which, if we grasp, can teach us who we are. You might fall in and out of love at the drop of a hat and think that therefore your "feelings" mean nothing, since you can apparently love someone one week and three more people in succession within a month. Below and behind all that flighty love, however, a gut feeling can emerge, telling you that you aren't ready for commitment to one person, that real, mature love is still a way in the distance. And if you listen to such feelings as this, you'll be more honest with yourself now and more honestly ready for better things to come. Having said that, I think we ought to get on the road toward new possibilities.

CHAPTER VI

DEVELOPING PERSONHOOD

For everything there is a season, and a time for every matter under heaven:
a time to be born . . . a time to keep silence . . . a time to speak . . .
a time for peace . . .

Honesty in New Relationships

Speaking of relationships in the last chapter, I mentioned the harm that could be done if one person tries to be too independent of the other, or indeed of all others. Yet a kind of independence is needed before any of us can rejoin the world after divorce and its turmoil. We have to make friends, go out on dates, get involved with others in the church support groups—yes. But in doing these things, we have to be sure we are gaining understanding of ourselves, a sense of what the psychologists call "personhood," so that we don't desperately need anyone else to give our lives meaning. Building relationships is a risky business because, as we have seen, we're yearning for affirmation and love. We don't perceive others' intentions clearly, or we mistake our own feelings about people we meet and misjudge the impression we're making on them. Maybe much of our problem stems from being in too great a hurry to get back to "normal." So we hurt others and ourselves, sometimes seriously; or we even get married too soon, hoping that will solve the problems. We ought to go slow. We ought not to take any serious steps toward the "rest of our lives" without first centering ourselves and finding significance in ourselves, alone. The sense of self, of personhood, will make the future possible.

It's good to be kind to ourselves and others. It takes time to find out "who I am." Give yourself time: make friends, not commitments you won't be able to live up to; take risks and experiment, but don't make promises you won't be able to keep. Be forgiving of yourself and of others caught up in this mess, realizing that they're going to be a little crazy, too, and make mistakes of their own as they look for the "ideal mate" to solve their problems.

Be honest with yourself and others. But how? Some of us want too much to be nice and not hurt anybody. Some of us want to keep all our options open. Some of us need to get affirmation and affection from the whole world. So we say nice things and appear interested when we're not. Or we string people along just in case the relationship we really want doesn't work out. Or we collect friends and acquaintances who gratify our egos. Maybe we don't do any of this consciously. We don't mean to manipulate others, but we do want to explore possible relationships. A thin line separates the two kinds of interacting, and we might not even notice when exploration stops and manipulation begins. This line is easier to recognize if we take the time to know ourselves and be sure of our identities first.

But at some point you could recognize in yourself a vague feeling that something isn't right between you and one or more of the people you're trying to relate to. You may feel enervated instead of uplifted after spending an evening with someone. You may not feel at ease with people you used to enjoy and even find yourself wanting to avoid them. Those are signs that something dishonest is creeping into the relationship, and you have to face the feelings and work through them carefully. First ask yourself what it is you wanted from a relationship that's now making you uncomfortable, whether you still want those things, or whether your attitude has changed. Then take into account the needs of the other person insofar as you can know them. And with kindness and consideration and gentleness—to both of you—do something to bring the vague feelings into the light of day. Discussion might clear the air and let you get started on a new and different footing with each other. Or it might end with a mutual decision to break things off.

What we don't need is continued unsatisfactory relationships because we can't face ourselves, or because we feel so wounded from our divorces that we think it's somehow justifiable to get back at others. Some of us unconsciously want to hurt all men or all women because of what our former spouses did to us. We take perverse satisfaction in getting revenge on surrogate "spouses" by hurting people we never knew before. This, of course, only hurts innocent victims and demeans us in our own sight. It also can start a vicious cycle in which we attract the kinds of people who will become appropriate scapegoats by fulfilling our expectations of what "all men" or "all women" are like, and then punish them accordingly. This is a severe example of patterns in our lives that honest, clear perception of who we are and what we want can change.

Something else we don't need in this delicate process of developing new relationships, both friendly and romantic is more guilt and self-hatred in ourselves and more blame for the rest of the world. So we have to *do* something if we find ourselves in an "unbalanced" relationship, where one likes and the other loves, where one is interested and the other not, where one wants full commitment now and the other wants to go slow. We've seen before how these situations produce tangled emotions of desperation, rejection, and worthlessness in the disappointed partner, and feelings of being trapped or of guilt over causing pain in the person who is more detached. But the imbalance of love has to be reckoned with sooner or later, and sooner is better. A clean break is also better than continually chipping away at each other (and I say that even though I hear you telling me it's all easier said than done). We will all say or do things in relationships which we later regret. We'll all have feelings which we find don't stand the test of time, or of close proximity either. But we can't let those inevitable mistakes, which are part of the process of learning to live with ourselves and with others, draw us back into old patterns of self-recrimination, guilt, and blame. Instead of stewing around berating ourselves for our mistakes, we should get out of them with some good, honest words and actions and get on with living a new and better life.

Mature Singleness

Hindsight gives us our best perspective on the dynamics of building relationships. Something we discover is that we too often expected the right thing from the wrong person. We might look back over several years of dating and of fleeting relationships only to realize that we were desperately seeking salvation in some other person outside ourselves. That quest ultimately failed because no one can save us but God. In practical terms, this realization means that we have to learn to look to God and to our own selves for the resources to be able to grow, really. Only the relationship between God and us gives us the maturity we need to survive and thrive in our new human relationships and patterns of living.

Thus the ideal time for a new relationship is when we feel honestly that we could be happy alone for the rest of our lives. This wouldn't mean that we would want to be alone, but simply that we would know we could live productive and peaceful lives without needing another person around all the time. We are then ready for a relationship that will last. Before that time we are searching and questing for an elusive goal that is not possible to achieve. No one—absolutely no one on the face of the earth—can make us happy but ourselves. If we are not content and solid within ourselves, we aren't the sort of person who could sustain a relationship with another mature adult human being. This may sound idealistic, but I believe it is true. We can't have good relationships when we're desperate. We have a paradoxical situation here in that many divorced people are desperate, and thus are not really willing to settle down to their own personal development. We want gratification now; we want to have the human nurture and support we have been missing. But we have to allow God first to help us find the unique person God made each of us. Only then can we be ready to work on living in a full relationship with another unique person of God's creation.

How Long Will I Hurt?

One of the last questions, but not the least, I hear you asking is, "Will the pain last forever?" The answer is: yes and no. Some people make a big deal out of telling us to let go of our self-pity and suffering, as if the pain were something we could voluntarily drop by the wayside and move on. Well, the fact is that we cannot will pain away. We can't make it evaporate overnight. We do not, after all, manufacture our pain in the ordinary sense of that word. At some points, we might "wallow" in it; but, at least in the early stages, our feelings are so raw and so changeable that we don't create them by will and we certainly can't remove them by an act of the will. This doesn't mean that we are helpless, but it does mean that the American view of will power is exaggerated.

There are times that the pain—whether of loneliness, perplexity, guilt, restlessness, or despair—seems to go on for ever and ever. Different people have different reactions, and I'm not giving a timetable. However, there's a general feeling among a lot of divorced people that the first year is the most miserable, and the pain is most intense then. During later times, the feelings will return and haunt us, as small things make us hurt for a longer period of time than they did before our divorce. We're not as resilient, but we are more alert to the hurts of others and ourselves. The sense of pain may come in waves, particularly around times like holidays or anniversaries when we'll feel especially down. It may well be that five years after our divorce we will have a day or two or even a week when the pain is intense. But we probably won't be immobilized, and we'll be able to work and live in a more or less "normal" way.

We know the pain goes on, not really without end, and yet not really under our control. For this reason, I've wanted throughout these pages to emphasize that the way to deal with the feelings is to confront them directly and work through them, not to try to evade them. This slow process requires devotion and effort, but we will reap benefits from the energy we have expended.

Lessons I've Learned

I promised early on that this would be "Lewis Rambo's book," and it seems to me that the best way to end it would be to share some of the rewards I've gathered from working through my divorce and from writing this book. I've learned some very specific things about myself. First, that ambition was the ruling theme of my life, and that ambition led to my working too hard in the wrong way and with the wrong results. Behind my quest for spectacular achievement in my vocation lay my very low self-esteem, which made me want to do great things and be famous, but paradoxically made me afraid to risk failure by being innovative or creative in my work. I stuck with technical scholarship and became a workaholic doing critiques of other people's work, while not taking the risk of putting my own ideas on the line. I was "productive," but not creative, so I was safe and protected from criticism. I worked all the time, felt guilty about not being creative, but assuaged the guilt with thoughts of how hard I was working.

Closely related to this pattern of activity in work was a pattern of interaction with my wife that led directly to the death of my marriage. I was afraid of genuine intimacy and commitment, afraid of putting myself on the line with my wife in my marriage, as I was of putting my professional self on the line at work. My wife and I both made attempts at love and did indeed love each other on many levels. But I resisted her love, and at last my immaturity, irritability, and workaholism drove her away. In the past, I would have been depressed by such an enumeration of my faults. Now I'm liberated by it, because I know I'm not just "guilt-tripping," but constructively and critically appraising my life. This gives me hope because I have new things to work hard on, new patterns to make part of my life. That is a challenge, but I'm now assured of the love of God, and even though there are times when I'm desperate or impatient, I know that God will sustain me and forgive me in spite of my rebellion, stubbornness, and arrogance.

I have also learned some more general lessons from my divorce and the subsequent struggle to maintain my faith and reconstruct my own life. The first is that God is not limited by our rules and regulations. God's love is majestic, vast, embracing. God comes to us in times of despair, to support us and to love us even when we are rebelling against the mercy and love of God. I think we sometimes make our churches so narrow and legalistic that we refuse to allow God to be God, or to allow for the full compassion and kindness of God to reign in our midst. Some churches are so concerned that their members be technically correct in behavior and belief that the church forgets its mission to serve and forgive those who are broken—in this case, the divorced. There's an antiquarian streak in some churches: they want to create a perfect church by following the Bible meticulously. Instead, they are like builders of perfect miniature model trains which are beautiful to behold and play with, but of little value as vehicles of transportation to real people in the real world. These "toy" churches are severely limited in the face of massive problems in the world. I don't mean to be harsh, but the fact is that Christians limit and manipulate God when by their actions they keep those who aren't "respectable" out of the church.

I've also learned that besides being majestic—the King of kings and the Lord of lords—God is a fellow pilgrim and fellow sufferer in Christ. It was the incarnate Son of God who said from the cross, "My God, my God, why have you forsaken me?" We often say that and feel guilty. Christ has lived through despair and suffering and is *with* us (not just "like us") in our times of death and crucifixion. And when we see Christ's suffering more clearly, we also appreciate the meaning for us of his resurrection. The power of Christ's resurrection is visible in our own healing, forgiveness, and hope. Thus his life and ministry and glory are no longer abstract theological affirmations, but living realities for us as we struggle, die, and are reborn in the image of Christ.

I have come to understand better the importance of the church's role as a community for friendship, support, and edification. We can't be Christians alone. The church has to learn to minister to the divorced. If we cannot find the love and forgiveness of Christ in the church, where else will we find them? I am grateful to the congregation to whom I have been preaching for four years. They were kind to me and did not force any legalistic issues on me. They trusted me, indulged me when I poured out my sorrows on them, and have given me the freedom to explore the meaning of the will of God in the midst of the pain of my divorce. They have also been open to the new insights I've discovered and haven't sought to stifle growth and development in themselves. In them I think I see what the churches of Christ are supposed to be.

Another lesson for all of us—but one that can be expressed only in very personal terms—is the importance of friendship when we are in trouble. A number of friends gave me unlimited love and support during the trauma of divorce. They loved me and helped guide me through, and I believe they were gifts from God to me. These friends made my life possible during the last three years. In crisis, we find out that friendship is one of the great joys and consolations of life.

The experience of divorce has also taught me that faith is a pilgrimage and an adventure, not just a rational or emotional assent to propositions about God, Christ, or humanity. Faith is a living relationship that embraces God, Christ, Holy Spirit, and the communion of saints. God's gift of faith lets us know the full range of human experience, from the heights of joy and praise to the depths of suffering and even the pit of doubt and despair. Most divorced Christians agree that during our trials and tribulations the book of Psalms supports us and our faith. The Psalms illustrate and illuminate the whole range of emotions we have to express and come to understand. Our feelings of rage and anger, our sense of loneliness and isolation, piercing guilt and hovering doom—all these human realities as well as joy, freedom, and forgiveness are portrayed with profound realism. We read the Psalms in the context of our own failures and frustration, and we know that faith is not a frail superstructure of defined beliefs, but first and foremost a relationship with a God who has lived among us in Jesus Christ, a God who is most clearly revealed to the meek, brokenhearted, and lost. Such faith lets us be angry with God and confess God and worship God in the full integrity of our own feelings, thoughts, and actions. Faith isn't easy answers, but nurturing on the pilgrim way. Faith isn't cold rationality, but living words that reveal and heal. (Since the completion of this book, I have read a marvelous book, *A Cry of Absence* [San Francisco: Harper & Row, 1983], by Martin E. Marty, which confirms and expands my own view of the Psalms.)

I have learned the lethal quality of a legalism that supposes guilt and innocence to be mutually exclusive categories. I cannot survive in a legalistic religious framework. No one can, but often people's lives seem to go on so well that they don't see the fragility of their religion and so live on from day to day in one dimension. Legalism doesn't work for people in a crisis like divorce. Cold reality shows us that everyone involved has sinned; nobody escapes pure and untainted. Even the "innocent" knows that he or she has violated the other person as well as the self and sinned against a loving God.

Perfectionism, I've also learned, stems from legalism—or they reinforce each other and make life equally impossible. The harsh rules and lack of a sense of grace in legalistic religion lead to self-destructive patterns in individual personalities and in social relationships. The idea that you can become perfect by perfectly following a clear set of regulations leads to the need to find a perfect mate and other perfect people to add up to a perfect life. You can't. Perfectionism paralyzes you because you don't want to make mistakes; it also gives you a harshly critical attitude toward others and yourself. To be human is to have faults, but perfectionists try to live life constantly disillusioned with themselves and disgruntled with other people.

I have begun to realize that the only way to survive a divorce is to find integrity in yourself and to live integrally with yourself. At some points, this may mean you are offensive, or apparently unloving, to others. But you have to be as honest as you can, first with yourself, then with God, and then with others. The last actually grows out of the other two, and makes for real compassion rather than fake "niceness." Seeing yourself, being your own and God's person, is a fearsome but ultimately liberating experience.

Finally, I've learned that life is both complex and simple. We can rarely find simple, clear-cut answers to problems—like divorce—that life poses for us. But paradoxically, life is simple when we believe and live in the belief that God is love; that redemption is in Jesus Christ; that faith is a form of life whereby God nurtures us and makes us able to live and serve with courage. Faith lets us risk living without being supported by simplistic formulas for our own actions or by attitudes of condemnation toward others. Life is full of hazards, but confidence in God lets us trust our ability to deal with the complexities of life, and to react authentically—from our own inner selves—to life's problems and vicissitudes. Knowing this, we can live for the glory of God and for the welfare of others.

TH DIVORCING CHRISTIAN

LEWIS R. RAMBO

"Rambo speaks confessionally about divorce, not hesitating to lay out his own experience as a divorced person. Yet, he is sufficiently through his grief process over the loss of his marriage that he speaks with an objectivity and clarity in giving substantive spiritual guidance and direction that at every point I find to be accurate, wise, and healing in their usefulness to Christians. He forthrightly deals with specific theological problems presented to Christians by their being divorced. His understanding of the church as a haven for hurting persons, a hospital for the wounded and brokenhearted, a community of wisdom, love, and support is the most valuable contribution of the book to the pastor and the lay person in the church. His other audience, divorced Christians, is his primary audience. He speaks to them directly and clearly in an empathetic manner."
—*Wayne E. Oates, Ph.D., professor of psychiatry and behavioral sciences; director, program in ethics and pastoral counseling, University of Louisville Health Sciences Center.*

For everyone who is experiencing the agony of divorce, *The Divorcing Christian* offers real hope and help. For the Christian, it can be a lifeline in a sea of guilt and despair. Reach out, and rejoice!

Louis R. Rambo is associate professor of pastoral psychology at San Francisco Theological Seminary and associate professor of religion and the personality sciences at the Graduate Theological Union at Berkeley. He also serves as minister of the Church of Christ in San Rafael. He is the co-author of *Psychology of Religion: A Guide to Information Sources.*

ISBN 0-687-10994-9   An Abingdon Press Original Paperback

BOOK DESIGN BY THELMA WHITWORTH